HOLY
Discontent

Books by Bill Hybels

Just Walk Across the Room
The Volunteer Revolution
Courageous Leadership
Rediscovering Church (with Lynne Hybels)
Honest to God?
Fit to Be Tied (with Lynne Hybels)
Descending Into Greatness (with Rob Wilkins)
Becoming a Contagious Christian
(with Mark Mittelberg and Lee Strobel)

The New Community Series
(with Kevin and Sherry Harney)
Colossians
James
1 Peter
Philippians
Romans
Sermon on the Mount 1
Sermon on the Mount 2

The InterActions Small Group Series
(with Kevin and Sherry Harney)

Authenticity	*Love in Action*
Character	*Marriage*
Commitment	*Meeting God*
Community	*New Identity*
Essential Christianity	*Parenting*
Fruit of the Spirit	*Prayer*
Getting a Grip	*Reaching Out*
Jesus	*The Real Deal*
Lessons on Love	*Significance*
Living in God's Power	*Transformation*

BILL HYBELS

HOLY
Discontent

Fueling the Fire
That Ignites
Personal Vision

ZONDERVAN.com/
AUTHORTRACKER
follow your favorite authors

This title is also available as a Zondervan audio product.
Visit www.zondervan.com/audiopages for more information.

Requests for information should be addressed to:

Zondervan, *Grand Rapids, Michigan* 49530

ISBN 978-0-310-28583-0

Global Trade Paper Edition

Interior design by Beth Shagene

Printed in the United States of America

08 09 10 11 12 • 23 22 21 20 19 18 17 16 15 14 13 12 11 10 9 8 7 6 5 4 3 2 1

Of the many joys in my life,
there are two that eclipse all others
and rise to a level that leaves this professional
writer/speaker close to speechless—
my two children.

●

Since the hour of her birth,
Shauna has held my heart.
And no son could make a father prouder
than Todd has made me.

●

Lynne and I regularly fall to our knees
and whisper our thanks to God.
This book is dedicated to them.

Contents

Acknowledgments / 9

Part I
Egyptian Slave Camps and Other Clever Hiding Places—
Where to Find Your Holy Discontent

1. The Question That Started It All / 13

2. Popeye People / 31

3. Your "One Thing" / 49

Part II
Three Counterintuitive Moves—
How to Develop Your Holy Discontent

4. Feeding the Frustration / 67

5. A Worthy Fight / 81

6. Wherever It Takes You,
Whenever It Takes You There / 99

Part III
Fanning the Flame —

The Key to Keeping
Your Holy Discontent Alive

7. Magnetic Living / 117

8. Hope's Purpose / 131

Postscript: It Doesn't Have to End Like This / 143

Notes / 151

Resources / 155

Acknowledgments

Some ideas burst into focus in a single moment. Others, however, are a little less cooperative. *Holy Discontent* required the gestation period of two full-term pregnancies, but fortunately, I had pastors from all over the world bear with me as I brought to life the book's core premise. I'm grateful to each of them.

When a publisher shows unbridled enthusiasm for a book about *frustration*, no less ... well, it must be a God thing. My heartfelt thanks to Team Zondervan.

And finally, I'm thankful for my ministry cohort and creative consultant, Ashley Wiersma, who assists me with books, conferences, videos, and any other projects that serve to move the kingdom forward.

Part I

Egyptian Slave Camps
and Other Clever
Hiding Places —

Where to Find
Your Holy Discontent

1

The Question That Started It All

The question had me vexed for two solid years. You probably know the type: questions like these keep you up at night, distract you when you're trying to stay focused on tackling other challenges, and cling to your last good nerve until they somehow get their answers. Here was the one that had disrupted my world for all that time:

What is it that motivates people to work where they work, volunteer their time to the groups they serve, and donate money to the causes they support?

That's it. That was my "vexing" question.

To put it simply, *Why do people do what they do?*

For starters, let's take the issue of vocation. Have you ever wondered why builders build, why writers write, why teachers teach, or why painters paint? I mean, what is it that compels people to give the vast majority of their waking hours to occupations such as these? Frankly, I think the answer is more substantive than merely "to get a paycheck" because an astounding number of us are also pouring time and energy into roles and responsibilities that don't pay a single dime.

In a given year it's estimated that American adults volunteer roughly 20 billion hours of their time. I have scores of friends in senior leadership positions with hospitals, ministry programs, nonprofit groups, schools, charities, and other worthwhile endeavors, and they all attest to the fact that their whole deal would crumble were it not for volunteer involvement. The annual dollar value on all that donated time, in case you're wondering, is about $225 billion[1]—roughly the total GNP of a country the size of Austria.[2] Add to that figure the many hundreds of millions in cold, hard cash that is given to worthy causes year after year after year, and things get pretty interesting.

With so many people engaging in so much positive, world-enhancing activity, the insatiably inquisitive part of my personality just wants to know one thing: *Why?*

As I mentioned, issues such as this one bounced around my brain unanswered for twenty-four long months. I started to wonder if I'd ever find resolution to it, but then came the welcomed breakthrough.

Moses' Underlying Motivation

Many people I know rely on various disciplines to help them gain a sense of peace or purpose as they get going each day. You probably have a few of your own, but one that I've tried to practice for several decades now is to read a small section of the Bible every morning. Admittedly, I don't always experience immediate dividends; on some days, I dutifully get through my fifteen minutes and then go about my life seemingly unchanged.

Then there are times when engaging in that simple practice serves to stretch my mind, infuse my heart with encouragement, and lift my spirit. The words seem to *leap* off the page!

This was one of those days.

I was making my way through the book of Exodus when I came upon an interesting passage about Moses, one of the greatest leaders the ancient world ever knew. You're probably well acquainted with his story; I thought I was too, actually, but what gripped me this time around was that I finally figured out the *underlying motivation* that fueled Moses' primary achievement in life—leading his people out of captivity and into the Promised Land.

Let me back up to the actual account, which begins in Exodus 2:11. The text says that "one day, after Moses had grown up, he went out to where his own people were and watched them at their hard labor."[3] (Quick note for context: Moses had been raised in Egypt by the pharaoh's adult daughter and was undoubtedly accustomed to the wealth, education, and freedom that accompanied such a privileged setting. Despite his posh Egyptian surroundings, though, Moses always knew that he was not *really* an Egyptian. He was Hebrew by birth—a Jew who was only living the Egyptian life "accidentally." So when the text refers to him seeing his "own people" working hard, it means his Hebrew countrymen, a group that at that time had been held captive by the Egyptians for more than four hundred years.)

Essentially, Pharaoh and his lieutenants were building a thriving economy on the weary backs of their Hebrew slave labor. The work ethic mandated by Egyptian overlords was merciless—day after day, Hebrew men with no rights and little hope for future freedom were pushed past the point of exhaustion in the sweltering midday sun as they made bricks for Pharaoh's vast construction programs. Moses' people had come to accept their plight as "the norm," believing there was nothing they could do to impact change.

It is in this context that we find Moses scoping things out around town, his heart understandably heavy as he sees firsthand the repulsive oppression his people were being forced to deal with. An already troubling situation takes a turn for the worse, though, when Moses looks up to find an Egyptian beating a Hebrew—one of his *own* people. Being treated as slaves was bad enough, but now his countrymen were being *physically* abused too? This level of injustice wasn't about to prevail on his watch! Moses has to do *something*.

•

Let me push Pause on the scene for a moment to ask you to consider the last time you saw a physical beating. I'm not talking about something you see in the movies that's been staged and scripted. I'm talking about a *real* fight ... up close and personal.

I hope you've never witnessed one; I've only seen one in my entire life, and I wish to this day I could kick the gruesome memory out of my mind. I was a teenager at the time, standing in front of my locker in the hallway of my high school in Kalamazoo, Michigan. Suddenly I heard some activity a few lockers down and looked up right as the awful situation unfolded. A young kid—probably a freshman—was minding his own business when a senior twice his size started to pick a fight with him. The senior was bulked up and had a snide grin on his face. He knocked the kid's books out of his hands and then totally humiliated him by yelling, "Pick 'em up ... NOW ! Pick 'em up!!"

He shouted loudly enough for the gathering crowd of students to hear, and when the tormented kid bent over to collect his scattered books, the bully started calling him terrible names, questioning his masculinity, and ridiculing him, his family, his upbringing, and whatever else he could think of. When the younger guy stood back up, his arms restrained by the heavy books he'd just retrieved, the bully wound up his right arm and threw punch after punch into the middle of the kid's face.

I can still hear the sound of the senior's fist cracking the nose and shattering the teeth of that young boy who was standing only a few feet from me. I can feel the hostility and rage in the air. I can see the thick blood splattering onto the light brown locker behind him and dripping onto the white terrazzo floor.

Although the whole thing seemed to have moved in slow motion, in reality it happened so quickly that none of us could do anything to stop it. Finally, three of my schoolmates lunged toward the bully and peeled him away before he could do any permanent damage to the freshman kid. It was a sickening experience—and unfortunately one I'll never forget.

Helping to Fix a Broken World

Beatings are *impossibly* tough to watch, and normal people don't soon forget the gruesome sights and evil sounds that accompany them. This is exactly the type of stomach-churning event that Moses is exposed to in Exodus 2 as he watches an Egyptian guy beat up a fellow Hebrew. He just can't bear the terrible sights, the heart-wrenching sounds, the splattering blood. The injustice of the situation is far too much for Moses to take, and suddenly, something inside him snaps.

The text says that upon "glancing this way and that"[4] and seeing no one around, Moses raced to the defense of his countryman. He grabbed the Egyptian and pulled him off his fellow Hebrew, which incited a fight of its own ... to the death. No doubt horrified by his capacity for violence, Moses buried the Egyptian in the sand and ran away.

The very next day, Moses went out to observe the plight of his people once again. What he saw must have shaken him to the core: now two Hebrews were fighting *each other*! Fists were flying, teeth were shattering, noses were breaking—these were the same sights and sounds as before! I bet Moses screamed at the top of his lungs, "Why are you beating up a fellow *Hebrew*? Did it ever occur to you that he's one of us? What are you *thinking*? Our people are in forced labor and are getting beaten up regularly by the Egyptians, and now, you're fighting with each *other*?!"

It was obvious to Moses that his people were imploding. They'd been exposed to such hatred and violence for so long that they'd probably just wipe *each other* out if left to their own devices. The appalling abuse and oppression and exploitation they had suffered under Egyptian rule had escalated to the level of total insanity, and Moses found himself on the extreme edge of his emotional limits. *"That's it!"* he must have cried. *"I've absolutely had it! I just can't stand this anymore!"*

●

Later in the book of Exodus, there is a famous exchange between Moses and God, which takes place beside a burning bush. Moses comes across a shrub that is on fire, but he notices that although it is burning, it's somehow not being consumed. Things become stranger still when he hears the booming voice of God calling his name. "Moses! Take off your sandals. The place where you are standing is 'holy ground.'"

As a kid in Sunday school, I had the distinct impression that the shocking sight of the burning bush that day utterly *scared* Moses into helping to free his people from Pharaoh's control. After closer study and reflection over the years, though, I've come to believe that the burning bush was simply an attention-grabber to get Moses to slow down long enough to hear God convey a level of empathy most of us never think to ascribe to him.

Suffice it to say, the bush-on-fire tactic worked, Moses cooled his jets, and God got the chance to be heard. I think his words to Moses went something like this: "Moses, I completely understand the rage you feel. I too have seen the misery of my people in Egypt. I too have heard them crying out. I too have felt their anguish as they suffer. What you saw when the Egyptian guy was beating the living daylights out of the Hebrew slave, and what you saw and heard when the two Hebrew guys were so frustrated, angry, and hopeless that they started beating each other—*I* saw those things too! And for what it's worth, I hate the sorrow and suffering as much as you do! More, actually.

"I am so stirred in my spirit, Moses, that I've decided to intervene from heaven," God probably continued. "I have chosen to rescue them, and I want to use *you* to help me![5] I've been looking high and low for someone *exactly* like you. If you will participate in my plan, then I will harness the internal firestorm that rages inside you and channel it into positive action—action that will help set my people free from their slavery.

"I'm going to assign you to a *specific* role because I see that you are as stirred up on earth as I am in heaven about this issue. I can see what this is doing to you on the inside! I see in you a passion for your people. In your raw emotion, I see a man with a *tremendous* capacity for activism—a man who refuses to stand by idly while his people are being so dreadfully mistreated. Your frustration can forge leadership mettle and fortitude in you, Moses, if you will let it."

That's All I Can Stands!

Keeping the Moses account in mind, I want to come at the dynamic I've been describing from an entirely different angle in hopes of anchoring a couple of key ideas in your brain.

I'm part of a generation that grew up watching a short, balding, mischievous cartoon character on television. His name was Popeye—Popeye the Sailor Man, to be precise, and if you're ten years on either side of me, you're probably humming the tune right now. Kids crowded onto family room couches every Saturday morning with rapt attention as the sailor with a corncob pipe and one good eye engaged in his next exciting adventure.

Popeye had a special girl in his life named Olive Oyl. She was a real traffic-stopper, as I recall. Flat chest, pickle-shaped nose, spaghetti-thin arms—quite the looker! Whenever someone cramped the style of his special "goil" as he called her, Popeye typically took it all in stride. He had a long fuse, and on most occasions, he was the epitome of calm, cool, and collected. But if things took on a menacing tone—if it looked like something *really terrible* might befall his beloved Olive Oyl, then Popeye the Sailor Man's pulse would race, his blood pressure would skyrocket, and his anger would begin to boil. He'd take it as long as he could, but once his long fuse burned up, Popeye would blurt out the words that an entire generation had branded into their psyche: "That's all I can stands, and I can't stands no more!" (Dubious grammar, I know ... what else would you expect from a sailor?)

The now-enraged Popeye would rip open a can of spinach and swallow the green lump in one giant gulp. Immediately, a stream of supernatural strength flowed into his body—mostly into his forearms. They'd instantly bulk up to quadruple their normal size, giving Popeye the strength to be an unstoppable force for good in the world. He'd crush the opposition in no time and save his precious Olive Oyl from all sorts of distress. Then, once life had returned to its steady state, he'd sing himself off the screen, "I'm strong to the finich, 'cause I eats me spinach ... I'm Popeye the Sailor Man!"

What a show!

●

As you'd imagine, people started eating a lot of spinach after that cartoon came out. But I think Popeye left behind a much more significant legacy than that, and it has to do with his key line, "That's all I can stands, and I can't stands no more!"

Friends, this is an *extremely* important line to think about!

What happens when we reach the point where we can't "stands no more"? Well, for our Old Testament friend Moses, he could no longer tolerate his fellow Hebrews being oppressed and beaten. He just couldn't *stand* it! It was his "Popeye moment," if you will—the final ounce of frustration that flung Moses right over the edge. Because God couldn't stand the Israelites' mistreatment either, he used what I call a "firestorm of frustration" that was brewing in Moses' soul to launch this unlikely leader into a prominent role that resulted in the nation of Israel eventually inhabiting the Promised Land.

Certainly, Moses is not the only person in history who was motivated by a Popeye moment to make a difference in the world. In recent days, I've asked loads of people I know to reflect on how *they* got involved in the things that now consume their time, their money, and their energy. What were the experiences that compelled them to pursue the passions they are now pursuing? Those interactions, along with some personal study and reflection, led me to craft a theory in my mind about this subject.

Here is what emerged: I believe the motivating reason why millions of people choose to do good in the world around them is because there is something *wrong* in that world. In fact, there is something so wrong that they just can't *stand* it. Like Popeye, they too experience a firestorm-of-frustration moment when they grow so completely incensed by the present state of affairs that they throw their hands up in the air and shout, "That's all I can stands, and I can't stands no more!" As a result, they devote their vocational lives, their volunteer energies, and their hard-earned money to making sure it gets fixed.

In my little straw-poll survey, the catalysts I uncovered that thrust people into their Popeye moments ran the gamut. A corporate executive I know had visited a ravaged third-world village teeming with starving kids and came away with an extra dose of compassion ... as well as fire in his gut to effect change. A young mom had battled through the pain of losing a baby and resurfaced determined to speak into the lives of other despondent women. A newly married couple had soaked up a news report on TV one night about an entire country filled with people who suffer under a corrupt political regime. Staring into the eyes of those who have no voice caused them to find their own in advocating individuals' rights in their spheres of influence.

The point is, the irresistible attraction to a specific cause that compelled these people to invest joyfully of their time, their money, and their energies always linked back to a single spark of frustration that fueled what is now a raging fire in their souls.

What Puts the "Holy" in Holy Discontent

I should clarify that the gory Egyptian murder scene and the wild burning bush episode weren't exactly why the words leaped off the page the morning I was doing my devotional reading in Exodus. I think the real reason I was so fired up that day was because I finally had some supernatural sustenance to feed the vexing question I'd wrestled with for two years. Based on the Moses account, my "firestorm of frustration" theory was starting to hold water. I mean, here you have a massive, history-altering turn of events that gets the Hebrew people freed from hundreds of years of spirit-squelching slavery, and yet the whole deal can be traced back to a simple alliance between God and one normal, everyday, earth-bound human being who happened to find himself stirred up by the exact same thing that stirred the heart of his Creator.

I've come to refer to the powerful, spiritual congruence that connected Moses' priorities to the priorities of God as his "holy discontent," and it's a concept that works in our modern world as well. Still today, what wrecks the heart of someone who loves God is often the *very thing* God wants to use to fire them up to do something that, under normal circumstances, they would never attempt to do. Whether you're a high-powered marketplace person, a stay-at-home mom, a full-time student, or something altogether different, you (yes *you*) can join God in making what is wrong in this world right! And it all starts with you finding your holy discontent; it begins with you determining what it is that you just can't stand.

●

Even the most optimistic people I know agree that there is plenty wrong in our world today—and the Bible would support them. Passages like Romans 8:20–21 tell us that the entire creation is frustrated, but that by God's power, everything that is broken and frazzled and wrong will one day be redeemed. In fact, if there's one thing that God is focused on every moment of every day, it is this idea of *restoration*. He is working right this minute—even as you are reading this sentence—to call our sorry and broken world back to its original beauty and purpose.

If you expose yourself to all that's broken in our world but neglect to view the brokenness from heaven's perspective (which promises that everything is in the process of being restored), then you'll get sucked into an impossible, downward spiral of aggravation and anger. Things will seem so bleak that you'll wind up taking up residence inside your firestorm of frustration instead of allowing it to propel you toward positive action.

Once that frustration and anger is understood as being your *holy discontent*, though—your spiritual connection to the God who's working to fix everything—it's as if an enormous wave of positive energy gets released inside you. Much like Popeye in his spinach-infused state, you become an *unstoppable* force for good in the world. This energy causes you to act on the dissatisfaction that's been brewing deep within your soul and compels you to say yes to joining forces with God so that the darkness and depravity around you gets pushed back. This supernatural supply of energy allows you to move forward past all the natural human-nature responses and enter instead into a life viewed from God's point of view. In other words, your perspective shifts from that which your eyes can see to that which God *tells you is true*. And it is in *this* reality that what is enslaved can still be set free, what is broken can still be mended, what is diseased can still be restored, what is hated can still be loved, what is dirty can still be made clean, and what is wrong can still be made right.

Truth be told, the most inspired, motivated, and driven people I know are the ones who live their lives from the energy of their holy discontent. They have a constant awareness that what is wrecking them is wrecking the heart of God. Refusing to *stay* fed up, though, they instead get *fueled by* their restless longing for the better-day realities God says are coming soon. They listen to the soulish instinct inside them that says life just doesn't have to be the way that most people experience it. Most importantly, they suit up and jump into the game when God says, "If you'll hook up with me, I'll involve you in effecting some much-needed change around here!"

●

There's another common denominator I've noticed in people who live from the energy of their holy discontent: not only do they hold fast to a "restoration perspective," but they also remember that *people* are among the things being restored. This should make perfect sense, since you can't genuinely align yourself with God's priorities and then traipse around destroying the crown of his creation, his people. The God I know cares deeply about people, so if your area of dissatisfaction doesn't also reflect an abiding concern for the protection and development of *all* people, then your frustrated ranting and raving is probably more of a glorified gripe session than the byproduct of a God-given holy discontent.

Part of living with God's perspective is remembering that the people you bump up against every day are "in process." If God has his way, every last one of them will be restored, redeemed, remade for his eternal glory. Think of all the times in Scripture when Christ made a way for people to get freed up from whatever it was that enslaved them, be it physical bondage, emotional bondage, financial bondage, sexual bondage, or any other kind of burden that left them feeling hopeless and oppressed. When Jesus Christ ministered here on earth, he said that if you know the Truth, the Truth will set you free.[6] In other words, by knowing and walking with Christ, people can be freed from *anything* that has them tangled up. It was true for first-century believers, and it remains true for us today.

What's more, once you choose to walk in the Truth, you get to be an agent of freedom in the lives of other people. I think that's why God makes freedom available as soon as you trust him ... so that you can receive it, live it, and then go impart it to someone else. Your ability to detect and then act on that which makes you discontent can actually *catalyze* freedom-based living in the hearts of your friends and family members! This is an idea I'll address more thoroughly in chapter 7, "Magnetic Living."

What About "Being Content"?

On occasion, when I engage people in discussions about this subject matter, I get the question, "Yeah, but what about all the voices that tell me to 'be content'?" It's true: much has been written and preached over the years advocating *contentedness*. Especially in religious circles, it seems there is a constant drumbeat for "finding contentedness" and for "being content."

Don't get me wrong, the motivations behind the theme are usually pure: in various places in Scripture, Jesus himself says to be *content* regarding how much money you have, to be *content* about your circumstances (even when they're not so great), and to be *content* when your basic needs like food and water and shelter are met.[7] I just happen to think there's another side to the equation. Friends, the trouble with contentedness is that, when lived out in isolation, it can be lethal! If you're not careful, you will become lulled into a state of satisfaction, safety, and serenity, and you'll altogether neglect needs in the world that should elicit *deep discontent* when you see them going unmet.

You can't read the New Testament without seeing some of these "discontentedness-producing" issues crop up. Questions like:

What about the poor?
Who will care for the sick and dying?
Will anyone visit prisoners?
Who will clothe the naked?

Or take in the orphans?

Or listen to the hurting?

Or give water to the thirsty, food to the hungry, and
community to the outcast?

I think it's entirely possible for us to rest in God's promise of a better day—one in which there will be no compassion fatigue, no antidepression pills, and no grumbling bellies in South Asian kids—while we work our tails off to usher it in!

In fact, I think that when you choose to live out of the energy of your holy discontent—elbowing your way past the troubles and struggles and injustices surrounding you in determined pursuit of the "better things" God has promised in his restoration plan—all of heaven rejoices! In the midst of the celebration, God probably looks over at the angels, who are all whooping and hollering in excitement, smiles a knowing smile, and says, "Looks like we've got another Moses on our hands...."

Popeye People

The American Red Cross reports that in the year 2005 alone they responded to more than 70,000 disasters.[1] When hurricanes pummeled Gulf Coast states, they were there. When tornadoes uprooted families, they were there. When wildfires consumed entire neighborhoods, they were there. They were *everywhere*, it seemed. But what's most intriguing to me about the Red Cross's constant presence is that the "they" who are constantly "there" are nearly always *volunteers*. Almost a million of them each year, in fact, which means that every single day, more than three thousand people invest their valuable time in this organization's efforts. And the Red Cross is just one organization out of literally *thousands* that are volunteer-driven.

To this issue, I've often wondered what happens in the souls of otherwise rational human beings that would cause them willingly—even *joyfully*—to sign up for high-challenge, high-risk, high-stakes endeavors in this world. Especially when they're not receiving a penny in return.

Pursuing Our "Ought-ness"

Martin Luther King Jr. became famous because of what he couldn't stand. A pastor by occupation, he wound up being one of the greatest volunteers the world has ever known. The racial oppression he saw all around him in the United States in the 1950s and 1960s ripped him apart: he couldn't stand the "Whites Only" signs on drinking fountains and bathrooms and doors to restaurants; he couldn't stand the fact that blacks, by law, were pushed to the back of the bus or forced to give up seats altogether so that white patrons could sit down; he couldn't stand the reality that his people were always found at the end of the receiving line for educational, employment, and housing opportunities.

He wanted the lynching of black people to stop. He wanted segregation banished. He wanted justice to be served so that his kids could grow up in a different world than the one he was living in!

The day finally came when that which King *couldn't stand* simply got the best of him. The holy discontent he felt in the depth of his being brought him to the point where he must have said in the privacy of his own soul, "God, that's all I can stand. I can't stand any more." It was this Popeye moment that launched King's movement toward racial equality.

King lived the rest of his brief thirty-nine years with ravenous passion for seeing a new civilization ushered in—one characterized by nonviolence, freedom, and justice. He was awarded the Nobel Peace Prize at the University of Oslo in 1964 for his tireless efforts to that end, and during his acceptance speech, he said, "I refuse to accept the idea that the 'is-ness' of man's present nature makes him morally incapable of reaching up for the eternal 'ought-ness' that forever confronts him."[2] Friends, *this* is what it looks like to live from a place of holy discontent—where *ought-ness* simply overtakes *is-ness*.

Martin Luther King Jr. knew that his activism would probably cost him his life. Tragically, outside a Memphis hotel one evening in April 1968, it did. I tend to think that the holy discontent that had taken up residence inside him simply wouldn't allow him to give anything *less* than his entire life—mind, spirit, soul, and body—for such a worthy goal. The sniper took King's life, but he couldn't take the astounding legacy of a man so committed to his mission.

It's the type of legacy I hope some of us will leave too.

To come at this idea with our "Popeye question" in mind, I wonder if *this* is what you can't stand—people being sidelined, treated as second class citizens, made to feel *less than* or nonessential to the world, just because of something as trivial as the color of their skin. Can you not *stand* to see favoritism or elitism or snobbery in places that claim to care about *all* people?

What can't you stand? Perhaps another example will help you clarify your own answer.

Saint of the Gutters

When you think of people who experience anger-inducing "firestorms of frustration," your mind probably doesn't rush to Mother Teresa. But even the most tender, compassionate people can feel an enormous sense of discontentedness when the right situation warrants it. CNN once quoted Mother Teresa as saying, "When I see waste, I feel *angry* on the inside. I don't approve of myself getting angry, but it's something you can't help after seeing Ethiopia!"[3]

Whether she found herself in eastern Africa or poverty-drenched India or on 137th Street in the South Bronx, no task was beneath her if it meant injecting a little hope into someone's life. Throughout most of her life, she could always be found holding the hand of a terminally ill person, or escorting wayward street children to safe houses, or cleansing open sores of lepers, or amassing funds to feed disease-riddled and bloated-belly people living in developing countries.

For the twenty years prior to her work as a world-renowned friend to the friendless, though, the young woman born Agnes Gonxha Bojaxhiu was just an average geography teacher who worked in Calcutta. This is where her Popeye moment comes in.

Each morning, she'd make her way to St. Mary's High School to inspire young minds, but all around the school, conditions were anything but inspiring. Life on the streets was deplorable! Her route to work took her right by men and women who were homeless, destitute, and incapacitated by disease. Every day, something in her spirit would cry out, "That's all I can stand! I just can't *stand* this anymore!" Ultimately, though, the gut-wrenching poverty that assaulted her senses and wrecked her soul day in and day out thrust her into solution mode.

Almost immediately following her "firestorm" experience, Mother Teresa secured the necessary permissions to quit her teaching job, rallied a few of her former students, and set about the work of rescuing men, women, and children who had been rejected by local hospitals and were literally dying on the streets. Initially, all that this ragtag team of do-gooders could afford was a small, rented space where they would administer care. Still, the warm room was a vast improvement for the folks who'd been lying in open sewers the day before. (Future supporters affectionately dubbed her the "Saint of the Gutters" because of how she got her start.)

In 1950, shortly after she had left the teaching profession, Mother Teresa received permission from the Vatican to launch her very own order, now known as Missionaries of Charity. I read recently that what began with a dozen or so people now has more than four thousand nuns who are all working diligently to ensure that refugees, alcoholics, victims of epidemics, drug addicts, prostitutes, the homeless, the blind, the disabled, the deaf, the poor, and the destitute are being cared for.[4]

But more incredible than the widespread influence of this group is the fact that it can all be traced back to one woman who just couldn't *stand* the idea that anyone—even the poorest of the poor ... *especially* the poorest of the poor—was living without hope and dying without dignity. Mother Teresa didn't devote herself to this cause because of a fat paycheck every month; she served the under-resourced people in her midst because her holy discontent had her by the throat and wouldn't let her go.

When people are struggling and there's nowhere to turn for help ... when kids are left parentless, adults are left homeless, families are left without food and water ... when disease-infected patients are tossed out with yesterday's trash ... is *this* what you can't stand?

The Promise of Promiseland

Volunteerism in any context is laudable, but if you want to see it play out with crisp, clean, high-definition clarity, there is no better place to look than inside the local church. This idea of finding and using your gifts for humankind's greater good ranks up there as one of my all-time favorite subjects to talk about for one primary reason: there is no faster track to your soul finding satisfaction than on the path of servanthood. When you throw a serving towel over your arm and get your life wrapped up in some aspect of kingdom-building activity that truly fires you up, you leverage your holy discontent in the rawest, most unadulterated way possible.

To refresh my awareness of how this dynamic works, I did something a few months ago I hadn't done in a long time: I took the "Promiseland Tour."

Promiseland is Willow's children's ministry, and the thirty-minute tour gives you a behind-the-scenes look at all the secret stuff that goes on while parents are in the large auditorium attending the weekend services. I wasn't preaching that weekend, and the minor role on the main stage I did have occurred near the beginning of the service. I took advantage of the opportunity to sneak out and see how things were going in kidville.

A security person and I weaved our way through the atrium and down the two flights of stairs that led to a brightly painted check-in area. We were immediately greeted by three cheery faces, all of them belonging to volunteers. One of them proudly said that she'd be more than happy to show us around.

We were first taken to the area designated for infants, where I saw men, women, and teenagers holding babies, rocking babies, and peeking down on babies who were sound asleep in their cribs. The environment was peaceful, warm, and inviting—and also run entirely by volunteers. We left there and walked a hundred feet or so to the "toddler" area, where things weren't quite as peaceful. Still warm and inviting, but with an unmistakable dose of two-year-old energy in the air.

I couldn't help but notice the inspired kids and thankful parents and engaged workers all around me. Everyone looked so happy! (Except the new volunteer in a suit and tie who had just gotten puked on. Evidently, somebody forgot to tell him that children's ministry work should never be approached without battle fatigues.)

I'd probably witnessed firsthand at least four dozen men and women fulfilling various roles that morning—all on a volunteer basis. As I reflected on that tour at a later time, I wondered about the firestorms of frustration that had prompted all of those volunteer workers to raise their hands one day and say, "Need help in children's ministry? Count me in! I'm ready to roll. "

For some of them, I felt sure that their holy discontent had been birthed in boredom. They couldn't *stand* going to church as a kid because the children's program was so atrocious. The presentation of God's good news was done carelessly, the workers were eighty-five years old and ornery, the cookies were stale, the playground equipment was no good, whatever. Suffice it to say, all that they remember from their experience as a kid in church is that they were *miserable*.

Somewhere along the way, they learned that relating with God is the grandest, most exciting adventure of life, but they never could forget those awful dog-years spent in the dark, lifeless basement of the church of their youth. This is why, when these people are presented with an opportunity to serve kids today, they pounce on it. *There's no way I'm going to let the children at this church suffer like I suffered*, they think. *No way ... not if I can help it.* And so they pour their mind, heart, and soul into rescuing young kids from the travesty of mind-numbing, insipid children's ministry.

For others, their holy discontent may have erupted when they discovered the prevalence of child abuse in this country. Based on statistics alone, they figured at least a small percentage of the kids in Promiseland had suffered abuse at some level. Sensing a firestorm of frustration welling up in their hearts and souls, they replaced their feelings of despair and hopelessness with *action*. They made childcare arrangements for their own kids for a few hours each week so that they could wrap loving, caring, and safe arms around a few kids at Willow who may have experienced dysfunction and violence at some point in their young lives.

Still others had reasons I'd never know. But they all rallied together under a common cause and were determined to make a difference. This is the promise of Promiseland, that children have a place of peace to call their own. That they will be accepted for who they are but also will be exposed to the truth about who they can be in Christ. That adults will engage in their lives rather than merely tolerate them ... or worse still, resent or abuse them. This remarkable ministry thrives in our church for one key reason: hundreds of men and women who just couldn't stand sorry children's programs refused to let their frustration fester but instead allowed it to fuel some life-altering action.

I think you know the question I have for you. *What can't you stand?*

●

It's true: the volunteers of Promiseland provide a fantastic picture of what it looks like to live out of the energy of holy discontent. As great as that program is, however, I have to admit that it's not unique. If you and I were to roam around Willow for a day, we'd find dozens of examples of this kind of volunteer inventiveness and dedication. We'd see CARS[5] ministry folks with their heads stuck under hoods and their hands busily working to get a Honda all fixed up for a single mom who's in dire need of transportation. We'd encounter AIDS board members and their teams of folks stuffing Hope Packs with toothbrushes and spiral-bound notebooks and clean T-shirts, all in an effort to bring some relief to families who live half a world away.

We'd come across finance council leaders, prayer team coordinators, and conference hosts ... groundskeepers, greeters, and elders, all of whom give themselves day after day, week after week, to work they love. And they do it free of charge.

Whether it's at Willow or at another local church or in a relief agency or in corporate America, I always feel a sense of awe when I see someone volunteering out of a state of holy discontent. I call it an "Acts 2" awe—remember how the early church felt as they saw the Holy Spirit's power and presence at work? In the words of one commentator, "Their hearts were hushed and subdued [as] astonishment filled their souls."[6] Very cool.

Truly there's nothing more inspiring than a person who transforms something he just *can't stand* into the kind of positive energy that advances restoration in the world. This is what's at work every time a check gets sent from a grateful heart to a worthy cause, all in the name of "doing good" in the world. It's what's at work every time a person steps into a church or a civic center or a relief agency's tent with an "I'm here to serve" attitude—and does so after logging forty or sixty or eighty hours at their "real" job each week. It's also what's at work when that real job is more than a path to a paycheck; it is an avenue for releasing a little pent-up holy discontent tension.

Holy Discontent at Work

Recently I accepted a speaking engagement with a group of Chicagoland physicians. Giving an "interfaith talk" to three hundred doctors can be a challenge in and of itself, but the ante goes up exponentially when the hospital system they all work for makes the one-day seminar mandatory for every physician in their network. I prefer it when audiences actually *want* to hear me speak, you understand.

The first half hour of the event was filled with announcements and regulatory updates delivered by official-sounding people who I'm sure had office walls full of degrees, certifications, and commendations. By the time I took the platform, every single lab-coat-wearing audience member was thumb-scrolling on a BlackBerry or sending text messages from a cell phone. If I hadn't been the guy tasked with summoning their attention, things probably wouldn't have seemed so depressing. As I begrudgingly took the ten or so steps toward the microphone, I fumed with silent regret over ever having agreed to help the hospital's president, a friend for years: he was the one who'd roped me into this commitment, and he was going to owe me big-time when it was all said and done!

I stalled for a few seconds by straightening my notes on the podium as I surveyed the crowd. Nobody looked up, but I'm not easily dissuaded. I cleared my throat and began my remarks. "Right off the bat, I'd like to ask you a question," I said. Still no attention was paid me. "Just out of curiosity, how is it that *you* wound up in the field of *medicine*?"

Finally, a few sets of eyes rose in my direction.

I focused on my small, new-found audience and continued. "You folks look like pretty intelligent people, but I know of about a dozen other professions that are a heck of a lot more lucrative and *far* less demanding than the one you are in. And so I just wonder, why *this* profession?

"Before I go on, let me say that speaking as someone who doesn't do what you do everyday, I marvel—absolutely *marvel*—at your ability and your desire to work countless hours each week to find solutions for people whose bodies are diseased, injured, mangled, and dying."

More heads popped up.

"I think that it must have been a *powerful inner force* of some kind that initially made you want to help people live healthy, functional lives. In fact," I continued, "if I had to guess, I'd say that the same, deep force must be the thing that sustains you even today, because what else could *possibly* be strong enough to triumph over all the obvious reasons for avoiding the politics, pressure, and heartache associated with a career in medicine?"

I let the thought sink in and in the brief moment of silence heard BlackBerries being set down and flip-phones snapping shut. For the first time that morning, I had their full attention.

"See, I have this theory," I said. "It's just a theory … you can take it or leave it. But here it is. . . ."

I laid out the entire "holy discontent" premise (Popeye and all!), and then wondered out loud if the bright men and women sitting in front of me perhaps delved into medicine because of one of these "firestorm of frustration" moments.

Maybe they had grown up in the care of a chronically ill parent or had seen a friend's body ravaged by Parkinson's or lupus or cancer. Maybe they'd conquered a disease in their *own* body and now wanted to help others to do the same. For some of them, maybe they'd lived in a place where they saw people suffer unnecessarily because medical attention was difficult or even impossible to come by. Still others may have had to bury a friend or loved one because of sloppy hospital procedures.

However they would define it, I was willing to bet that a high percentage of them had been through an undesirable situation or circumstance that caused them to rise up and say, "I just can't *stand* this anymore!" I knew that if they would think critically about that experience, they'd gain fresh insight into why they pursued a career in medicine in the first place ... as well as renewed energy to stay in the game from here on out.

●

I remember trying to make my way to the parking lot after that talk, but more than a dozen doctors blocked my path. My instincts about the firestorm theory applying to this crowd evidently had been right—every person in that little postgame mob was armed and ready to tell me the exact "Popeye moments" they'd experienced. Not surprisingly, they all remembered precisely where they were and what was going on in their minds and hearts when they first decided to fill out the med-school application that led them into this field.

I found it fascinating to learn what compelled those doctors to get up every morning and head to work, anxious to save another life, fight another disease, or bandage another wound. I find it fascinating to pose the question to almost anyone, actually. When I interact with teachers, I ask them what motivates them to fire up every day to shape young minds. I talk to firefighters and police officers and EMTs and probe why they give their lives everyday to dangerous and often life-threatening public service. I talk to public defenders and ask why they care enough to fight for the rights of people who can't otherwise afford representation.

I ask artists why they're so jazzed about painting or singing or dancing.

Vocationally, whether you are a retail manager, a day trader, a writer, a marketing director, a producer, a lawyer, a computer engineer, a truck driver, an administrative assistant, a grocery clerk, a professional athlete, a salesperson, or a small business owner, my question for you is the same: *What can't you stand?*

"Even If It Kills Me, These Kids Will Get Fed...."

Someone who was crystal clear on the issue of what he couldn't stand was Dr. Bob Pierce, founder of World Vision, one of the largest Christian relief and development organizations in existence today. I served on their board for six years and remember being deeply inspired by what I now would refer to as Bob Pierce's *holy discontent*.

In 1950, Pierce experienced a *massive* firestorm of frustration in his heart. He watched with disbelief as little kids who had been orphaned by the Korean War in third-world Asia dropped dead while standing in line for food. When Pierce went seeking answers as to why, he learned that there just wasn't enough food at the front of the food lines. In what I consider a dramatic "Popeye moment," Bob Pierce headed back to the United States, gathered his most affluent business partners together in a meeting room in Los Angeles, and together birthed the reality now known as World Vision. "We're going to get food at the front of the food lines," Pierce vehemently declared. "If it *kills* me, we're going to do it."

Truth be told, it almost did.

In the end, however, his persistence paid off. On one overseas visit, he had given all the money he had on him to a little girl named White Jade who came from a poor Asian family and who was beaten and disowned after announcing she had made a decision to become a Christian. His five-dollar bill was just enough to provide her with food, clothing, and schooling, and knowing that the one thing she needed more than anything was hope for the future, he pledged to send her money every month from then on. This small, seemingly spur-of-the-moment gesture served as the catalyst for what would become World Vision's elaborate child sponsorship program, now active in hundreds of countries all around the globe.[7]

Through World Vision's efforts in 2005 alone, more than 100 million people in ninety-six countries received physical, social, and spiritual support.[8] In other words, there is now food at the front of those food lines. Just think of the myriad White Jades whose lives have been *radically* enriched because of Pierce's determination! Here again, though, it all started with a single, heart-wrecking area of holy discontent that forced one man to get in the game.

An Audacious Vision

Billy Graham is another man who put his holy discontent to work. In the summer of 2005, people all across the globe cheered on the master evangelist as he spoke to nearly 250,000 people in greater New York.[9] If the event represents his "final crusade" as it has been touted, then it ends a *sixty-year* run of filling stadiums in every conceivable part of the world. It's a case of longevity that begs the question, *What must have been churning and burning inside young Billy that compelled him to rent that very first stadium in order to host his very first crusade where he asked people by the thousands to give their lives to God?*

Or to come at this from a "Popeye" point of view, what was it in those early days that Billy Graham just *couldn't stand*? Whatever it was, it must have been extraordinarily powerful because it would serve as the true energy source from which all the rest of his achievement would flow. It would drive him to give his entire life to pursuing an *audacious* vision. It would ignite his motivation for building teams, inspiring colleagues, showing up at revivals, and enduring criticism day after day, month after month, and year after year.

Personally, I think that Billy Graham just couldn't *stand* to see people go through life without knowing God's love. It's the primary theme of every talk he gives: "The Bible teaches that God is love," he says each time he takes a stage, "and if you don't remember anything else, remember this: *God loves you!*"[10] As a kid, Billy Graham says that he had his reality rocked when he came across a verse in the Bible that said to go into the entire world and tell everyone about God's love. From that moment on, he was a goner! His life's course was set, and he sold out mind, body, and soul, to the vision God had given him. More than 210 million audience members in 185 countries later,[11] I'd say he's fulfilled the mission.

I ask you again: *What can't you stand?*

Is it people living love-starved lives—never knowing that there is a merciful God who created them and wired them up in a unique way and has a plan for their lives here on earth? This was the issue that sparked Billy's firestorm of frustration. I wonder, does it have the same effect on you?

What can't you stand? I hope that by now you know your answer to this all-important question, because you will never make as meaningful a contribution as when you operate from the energy of holy discontent.

3

Your "One Thing"

Despite my well-architected argument dissuading it, I realize that it would be easy for you to opt out of the whole holy discontent deal right about now. You could claim that, try as you might, you'll just never be a Martin Luther King Jr. with a life story fascinating enough to land you in the annals of history. You'll never be as humble or saintly as a Mother Teresa. You'll never be as loving or resourceful as a Billy Graham. You'll never be as patient as a Promiseland worker, as visionary as a Bob Pierce, or as committed to the health of total strangers as the one who gladly endures years and years of medical training just to try to make them well.

I think it's quite natural to assume, in fact, that everyone who has *ever* made progress in repairing this broken world must have been smarter, stronger, richer, feistier, more talented, more ambitious, more energetic, more persistent, and far more creative than you. Again, it would be easy to opt out. It would be easy to talk yourself into believing that this "holy discontent" business is reserved for everyone else *except* you, but you, my friend, would be dead wrong.

●

During a weekend service at Willow last year, I did what I commonly do when I want to simplify something that's complex: I sketch it out. It's my own take on "modern art," if you will. Anyway, I was talking that weekend about how to know when a passion pursuit qualifies as a bona fide "holy discontent," and here's essentially what I drew on the flip chart:

I explained that the vertical tick marks across the center of the sheet represent the years of a person's life, and that the cross stands for the moment when someone turns over control of his or her life to the authority of Christ. In doing so, they determine to start living for someone other than themselves, they step into a whole new kind of life here on earth, and they secure their future in heaven with the God who makes this entire transaction possible. Pretty big decision, I'd say.

Then I posed a simple question to the people gathered there that night: "Have you ever wondered why, when you turn over your life to God, you don't just get express-freighted right to heaven? Or, to put it a little more crassly, if you're so *heaven-bound*, then why are you still sucking air down here?" (Creekers have come to expect this level of eloquence and tender-heartedness from their senior pastor.)

Although countless trees have been killed in the name of explaining this issue of "why we are here," I think there's a single verse of Scripture that sheds as much light on the situation as anything else. Ephesians 2:10 says that "we are God's handiwork, created in Christ Jesus *to do good works*, which God prepared in advance for us to do."[1]

We were all created to do good works. I was created to do good works. Just as confidently, I'm here to tell you that *you* were created to do good works, which explains how I know that you have a holy discontent banging around in your brain somewhere—if you're alive and kicking today, then there is a *specific work* that you are expected to do. There is a set of tasks with your name on it that God has given you to accomplish, and long before you actually arrived on the scene, God planted certain seeds in your soul that he remains whole-heartedly committed to watering, growing, and making into something meaningful, if you will let him.

The danger in opting out of the holy discontent pursuit is that in doing so, you also opt out of tackling the good works God has wired you up to accomplish. The goal, friends, is to cultivate your soul's soil so that this doing-of-good-works process can unfold in your life—or, as you might say, to *opt in*. There is no greater satisfaction this side of heaven!

Someone Just Like You

Let me offer a brief word about this "specific work" idea. While I believe that it is extremely important to pay attention to holy discontent whenever it occurs in your spirit, I don't believe that *every* time something affects you deeply, it automatically becomes your God-given calling or your divinely inspired, personal life assignment. You may find yourself affected deeply by all sorts of troubling situations in our world, but this does not necessarily mean you've landed on that *one thing* to which you should devote your entire life.

Here's how I keep it straight in my own mind. There is a verse in the Bible that says that once we turn our lives over to God, we begin the process of becoming "transformed into his image."[2] It's a long-term project to be sure, but over time, Christ-followers should in fact begin to look *less* like themselves and *more* like Christ. Therefore, on an ever-increasing basis, Christ-followers should be abandoning their self-seeking viewpoints and taking on heaven's perspective. They should be loosening the grip on self-centeredness and instead looking for ways to serve others. They should be resisting the temptation to judge and seizing more and more opportunities to give grace instead.

As God works in our lives, turning us into fully devoted followers of Christ and therefore into *progressively more compassionate* people, many of society's ills should break our hearts and prompt us to action of some sort. For instance, when we see a massive tsunami hit nearly a dozen countries and kill almost 300,000 people, we'd *all* better pray the prayers, write the checks, route the aid, and garner the necessary resources to ensure victims' needs are met. (Thankfully, in the days, weeks, and months since the horrifying tidal wave rocked the world at the tail end of 2004, millions of people have been doing exactly that.)

However, in addition to being moved toward short-term, "cause-inspired" action, I think you constantly should be on the lookout for that *one* cause or purpose or problem that grabs you by the throat and just won't let go. Your "one thing" is the stirring situation that causes so much damage to your soul that it brings you to your own Popeye moment—a place where you feel you simply *must* do something. Your "one thing" births a *burning-bush* experience in your soul where you sense God himself inviting you into an *intentional* and *personalized* partnership with him to renovate reality.

For Moses, it was protecting his people from abuse. For Bob Pierce, it was getting food at the front of the food lines. For Martin Luther King Jr., it was realizing racial reconciliation. For other people, it's other things.

The reason why it is so critical for you to dig in and figure out what it is that wrecks *you* is because you may be the one person God is looking for in order to reverse some ugly and destructive trends in your generation. In fact, when you find yourself standing on the sacred ground of your burning-bush experience, don't be surprised if you hear God say, "*This* is why I made you and why I wired you up like I did! This is why I allowed the mountain-top, reason-for-rejoicing times in your life, as well as why I let the pits of despair sneak in. None of your tears of anguish will be wasted; I plan to use *every ounce* of what you've been through for good in this specific area. I know you are devastated by the same problem that grieves me, and I just happen to have in mind someone *exactly like you* to help me solve this!"

Let me say that last part again. God is looking for someone *just like you*—someone who gets wrecked on planet Earth by the things that wreck him up in heaven—so that he can sign you up for service. I assure you there is a holy discontent with your name on it. There is something out there that God is waiting for you to grab on to so that he can use you to help solve it. It wrecks you, it wrecks him, and he is ready for you *both* to do something about it.

●

So, how will you know your *one thing* when it shows up? For starters, it will be the pesky preoccupation that vies for your undivided attention during the day and keeps you wide-eyed at night as it captures your heart and ignites your imagination. It will be the thing to force you to the floor, heaving sorrowful tears the whole way down. It will be the thing kicking and screaming inside you, squawking for all it's worth to be addressed. Perhaps your *one thing*—the foundation of your holy discontent—won't affect other people in the same way, but for you, it's devastating at a core level. Like my friend Max Lucado says, it's that "inner music" that no one else hears precisely the way you hear it.[3]

I wonder ... what is it for *you*?

Whatever your answer, your *one thing* will move you off dead center, get you off the couch, and thrust you into the game, where it's fight, fight, fight until some progress starts to show up! What's more, once you say yes to serving God's agenda in the world, he then begins the process of channeling the holy-discontent frustration into a positive vision that propels you into a future charged with energy and purpose. At some point along the way, you'll find yourself so astounded by the kingdom-oriented voltage coursing through your veins that you'll lift up your head and with no inhibition whatsoever shout, "I was born for this!"

Guess how I know.

A Personal Burning Bush

The last thing I ever wanted to be was a pastor. Folks at Willow Creek have often heard me describe how in my late teens I had my sights firmly set on running our family produce operation as soon as I finished my college studies. My father and his brothers had spent thirty-five years building the business, and the arrows of my life all seemed to be pointed toward my carrying the torch into the next generation. I had the work ethic. I had the business appetite. And soon enough I'd have a degree that reflected completion in all the right coursework—economics major, business administration minor. Everything was perfect! Except for one small problem: the church I was attending in those days was so unbelievably self-absorbed that it didn't give a flying rip about people who lived close to us but far from God. In my estimation, the church leaders and members *preached* compassionate love; they just didn't see the need to practice it.

The troubling trifecta of ill-planned church services, uninspired preaching, and a whole slew of Christians who weren't fired up about much of anything, wrecked me a little more each week, but I wasn't altogether sure what I was supposed to do about it. I stayed focused on my business classes and my business future, but all along the way, I noticed something tugging on my soul. Had I the vocabulary at that point to name it, I certainly would have recognized it as an early form of my holy discontent.

Even as a junior high kid, I remember driving home from church with my dad one Sunday after yet another excruciatingly boring worship service. He was explaining that a business associate of his named Bob was starting to show some interest in God and that he was planning to invite him to our church. Evidently, Bob's wife had recently been diagnosed with terminal cancer, and the news had thrown their entire family into a tailspin. According to my dad, even though Bob was living pretty far from God, he had been rattled enough by his wife's medical report that he finally was open to investigating spiritual things.

I can remember listening to this entire spiel as if it happened yesterday. Once I heard he was planning to invite the guy to church, I instinctively begged him to reconsider.

"Dad, whatever you do, don't invite him to our church! If there's *any* spark of spiritual interest in him, we'll extinguish it in sixty minutes flat! We'll chase him further away from God than he was even before his wife got that bad news. His only hope is to stay away from our church! You just *can't* let him come!"

My father smiled at my protectiveness for the spiritual future of his business friend, but I was doing a slow burn on the inside. Even at that young age, my holy discontent was being fueled.

A little later, when I was seventeen years old, I took the wildest kid in our high school to church. Actually, this schoolmate had *requested* to come—what else could I do but oblige him?

Sunday rolled around and brought with it a leveling one-two punch. The guy showed, and my church delivered as expected—sixty minutes of utter irrelevance. The experience *ruined* him. As far as I know, he never darkened the doorstep of another church again. But he wasn't the only one who had been damaged by the experience—it had damaged me too.

From there, my holy discontent continued to build until my business-minded college years, when I sat under the tutelage of Dr. B, the man who catalyzed my first Popeye moment. As Gilbert Bilezikian painted a vibrant picture of what a thriving, Christ-like church was supposed to look like, I couldn't help but cringe in my spirit. I knew I'd never been part of a community like that. More troubling still, I knew from firsthand experience that *countless* people in our surrounding neighborhoods desperately needed the infusion of life and hope and excitement that only a biblically functioning church could afford.

Finally! I had been given a clear vision of the beauty, power, and potential of the local church when the local church is working right. I knew then and there that my best-laid plans for business would dissipate into thin air. In the space of one class period, my applecart got completely overturned by the thought of seekers going to hell simply because Christians refused to break out of their holy huddles long enough to embrace them. That realization is all it took for me to scream out in my heart, "That's all I can stand, and I can't stand any more! Seekers *matter*. And people far from God deserve better local church options than the ones available to them today!" Clearly, starting a healthy, Acts 2 church was to be my life's "one thing."

My burning-bush conversation with God occurred when I was twenty-two years old. God said, "Bill, I'm going to turn your holy discontent—your firestorm of energy and frustration—into something positive. I know how much this issue wrecks you. And because it wrecks me too, I'm going to harness your energy and use you to *change reality* for those seekers. I'm going to give you a compelling vision for providing a place where *all* people—regardless how far they are from me—can be welcomed and encouraged and made better because of people close to me who genuinely care."

The next thing I knew, I was renting the nearby Willow Creek movie theater with money earned by selling tomatoes door to door (this is what sons of produce company owners do, I guess) and asking three of my buddies to help me start a church for unchurched people.

I've served as the senior pastor of Willow Creek Community Church for three decades, friends, and truth be told, the same holy discontent is what drives me to this day.

●

A few months ago, all of Willow celebrated the thirtieth anniversary. Lots of people said all sorts of nice things about the insight and courage it took to start the church, but in my heart I knew the truth. There was nothing nice or noble about my starting Willow: I simply had to do it! The holy discontent simmering deep inside would have cooked me if I hadn't moved to some form of activism in this area. The process nearly killed me, but even that price would have been worth it in order for seekers to be welcomed into our fellowship! The longer I serve, the more resolute I become that I wouldn't trade the satisfaction and joy I've received as a result of chasing down God's "good works" for me to accomplish for anything in the world.

An Unstoppable Force for Good

I'll leave it to you and God to discern what your "specific work" is all about, but as you sort out the issue, can I give you a few examples of friends of mine who are living out their *one thing*? Maybe it will spark something helpful in you.

I have a friend who is a retired airplane pilot, and early on in our relationship I learned that he had fallen away from God during his high school days—a decision that led to his choosing to head down some terrible, life-threatening paths in his teenage years. Later on in life, he surrendered himself to Christ—whole-heartedly this time—and learned that he could actually be useful in the high school ministry of his local church. For many years now, he has opened up his home every Monday night in order to cook a meal for a big group of students who convene week in and week out to enjoy fellowship and food with each other. He always refers to it as the best day of his week.

A married couple I know hates the fact that so many church campuses are minimally landscaped and rarely demonstrate the unparalleled beauty of the Creator. Twenty years ago, they took it upon themselves to design, plant, and maintain several flower beds that lead into the main entrances of Willow. They're still at it today.

There is a carpenter at Willow who has become a friend of mine. His dad was never around when he was growing up to care for the family or to fix what was broken around the house. His memories of that relational gap keep him fired up all these years later to offer free handyman assistance to a group of single moms in our church.

A woman I know went through a gut-wrenching and humiliating divorce several years ago and had nowhere to turn for help. She suffered through an agonizing process of recovery and now eats, drinks, sleeps, and breathes our church's divorce recovery ministry.

One dad in my circle of friends was neglected and thus hurt very deeply by an emotionally distant father. These days, he is a key player in our Dad/Son and Dad/Daughter sessions at Camp Paradise, Willow's retreat facility in the Upper Peninsula of Michigan.

A business guy I know made six figures a year but went bankrupt due to careless credit-card spending. He hated what that did to him emotionally and spiritually, but he also grew to despise the social stigma attached to "bankrupt" individuals. Once he was back on his feet, he learned about our church's "Good Sense" financial planning ministry and became a budget counselor to young married couples. Can you imagine how much joy he derives from telling couples, "I fell headlong into a terrible financial pit, but you don't have to! Let me show you the way."

●

Whether you've been walking around on this planet for eight years or eight decades, I *urge* you to reflect on the *one thing* in the world that wrecks you when you see it, when you hear it, and when you get close to it. Because your one thing is the *exact* thing that will create enough tension and angst, carve out enough capacity for activism, and stir up enough of an internal firestorm that you'll have no choice but to suit up and get in the game.

Is it injustice of some kind or extreme poverty or homelessness? Is it loveless marriages or abused children or the pandemic of AIDS? What about racism or immoral business practices or crooked politics?

I wonder what it is for you.

It could be dysfunctional or slowly dying churches, inwardly focused Christ-followers, or lackluster worship. Or it could be watching over-entertained and under-challenged young people—an entire *generation* of them—drift further and further away from God.

I recently learned of a couple in a one-traffic-light town whose two teenagers pushed back forcefully against going to church. Problem was, it was the only church in their area, and both parents strongly desired that their kids be involved in Christian community. They grew so weary of the week-in, week-out battles on the subject, but they didn't know where to turn. It was obvious that this little church was dying and that the youth program left a lot to be desired. One weekend, in a burst of insight, they asked their kids, "Is there *any* church you'd be excited about attending?" The church their teens cited was seventy miles north of where this family lived, and the high school group met on Wednesday nights—the worst possible time of the week for two busy professionals. How was *that* supposed to work?

The father wasn't surprised that his kids were drawn to this particular church: he had a medical practice in town, and several of his patients made the long commute each week because of the high-quality, high-energy, high-challenge programs offered. *I'm sick of begging my kids to like church*, he thought. *If they're fired up about a group that meets three counties from here, then it looks like we'll be road-tripping it for awhile.*

The following week, fueled by their shared Popeye moment, he and his wife bit the bullet, rerouted some discretionary funds, and rented a giant bus. "Get all your friends together," the dad told his kids, "and tell them to meet in our front yard Wednesday night at five o'clock. And tell them not to be late! I'll be chauffeuring, and I'll give you one guess as to where we're going."

"You're not serious," his son said.

"Yep. And I don't want any empty seats come Wednesday night." He was grinning, but his son had overheard a discussion involving the cost of the rental and knew he'd better fill the bus.

Wednesday came, and what a party it was for those kids! The three-hour round trip was one that those kids would never forget. How could they—that bus ride was the first of more than a *hundred* of them to come. Two and a half years after that initial decision, the doctor is still moonlighting as a bus driver every Wednesday night for about six dozen kids who otherwise would have remained spiritually sidelined for a long, long time.

Now, back to *your* one thing.

If you're alive as you're reading this—and I presume that you are—then God has a few good works for *you* to wrap *your* life around. Opt out, friends, and miss the most important opportunity of your earthly existence to be an unstoppable force for good in this world.

Part II

Three Counterintuitive Moves —
How to Develop
Your Holy Discontent

4

Feeding the Frustration

Now that you're all fired up about locating what it is you can't stand, allow me to be painstakingly practical for a few chapters and offer up some observations to help you manage your holy discontent once you finally discover what it is. The first is this: when you find your holy discontent, *feed* it!

I know that sounds counterintuitive, so let me explain.

The tendency for most of us when we encounter stuff that creates *dis*-ease and frustration in our souls is to push it away. And fast! We feel the discomfort of holy discontentedness coming on, and reflexively we want to medicate it. We want to recoil in disgust at the dreadful realities surrounding us. We want to head to Blockbuster to rent another movie just to stay distanced from it. But the truth is this: the best thing you can do is to move *toward* your area of holy discontent until you have clear direction from God as to what action you should take to resolve it. For example, if the plight of the poor becomes your holy discontent, then *increase* your exposure to the poor. I'm serious here: Move *toward* the poor, not away from them. Rearrange your life so you can see afresh the horrific conditions that some people are forced to live in. Embrace the uneasiness that enters in when you listen with unsullied ears to the frustration of those who are trapped in cycles of generational poverty.

Raw Passion and a Slingshot

One of my all-time favorite characters from the Old Testament is King David. He made quite a name for himself even before he held the title of King, mostly due to a well-known episode involving a monstrous man and a miniature slingshot. I love this story!

Here was this young, peach-fuzz-faced teenager who was asked by his dad one day to leave the flock of sheep he'd been watching and go take some food and supplies to his three oldest brothers who were fighting at the battlefront. Young David didn't necessarily expect anything dramatic to unfold; he was essentially the pizza delivery boy out for a quick drop-off.

As he approached, he heard a nine-foot-tall Philistine behemoth named Goliath trash-talking the beloved God of the Israelites, as well as the Israelites themselves. I can almost hear Goliath's denigrating comments now: "Your god is pathetic! Don't you realize what a small and impotent master you weaklings bow down to? Who's man enough to fight *me* one-on-one? *I'll* show you some power!"

Evidently, the ridicule had gone on for some time. First Samuel 17:16 says that "for forty days the Philistine (Goliath) came forward every morning and evening and took his stand." David hung around for three of those days and was forced to listen to this giant creep mock his God. Shocked and annoyed by the vulgar mockery, he finally looked at his comrades in camp and asked, "Hey, why doesn't anyone shut him up?!"

The guys surely thought David had a screw loose. "Um … because he's *huge?*"

Goliath's armor alone weighed twice as much as the scrawny kid. Still, the young warrior-to-be *refused* to stand by while his powerful God was derided. He knew his answer to the "what-can't-you-stand" question, and he was determined to do something about it! David approached King Saul to ask permission to kill Goliath on behalf of the entire nation of Israel. In essence, he said, "Lemme at him! I can do it! I've been taking care of my dad's entire flock of sheep for years. Whenever a lion or a bear snatched one of them away, I'd chase after it, grab it by its hair, strike the thing dead, and rescue the sheep from its mouth, no problem. And I plan to do the same to Goliath. I *have* to, in fact! You expect me to sit idle while he defames the name and character of our great God? All due respect, but no can do, Sir!"

I love the competitive spirit of this kid! Despite his youth, though, King Saul knew to take David seriously. If you study it carefully, I think you'll see why. Underneath David's words was the thumping heartbeat of his *real* declaration: "That's all I can stand, King Saul, and I can't stand any more!" Before it was all said and done, that young man's Popeye moment would make him crazy enough to run full speed ahead toward the giant Goliath with nothing but raw passion and a slingshot. (How rational was *that* move? He had no plan B. He barely even had the king's full support behind him. What David *did* have, however, was God's attention.)

God saw in David a holy discontent—a raw, unbridled passion to defend the honor of his countrymen. His fervor literally would change the world, along with a little supernatural aid from God, who turned a smooth stone into a laser-guided missile destined for a direct hit on Goliath's forehead. In my view, God never intended for Goliath to depart the victor; instead, he was waiting for *somebody* to step up and say, "What you care about, God, is what I want to care about too. What stirs your spirit, God, stirs my spirit too. And however you want to use me to help solve the problem that we both see ... I'm in!"

David was a guy who got all up in arms when it appeared the enemy was going to win the day. He just went *nuts* when oppressive personalities steamrolled vulnerable types. For him, sitting still would have been impossible when he saw a group of people being demoralized or made to feel small. And yet he didn't try to escape his holy discontent; instead, he ran straight toward it.

Friends, as difficult as it may be at times, you simply must follow suit. Run *toward* the giants that threaten to impede your holy discontent progress! Get *close* to your holy discontent because when you feed rather than flee it, God will birth new visions in you to become part of the solution. Stay near it so you can pick up fresh sights and fresh sounds that will stoke the firestorm of frustration in your soul. Why? So that God will have a topped-off energy supply in you to use in doing some seriously *positive* things in the world! Trust me: this stuff won't happen on its own. If you want to be a force for good, then, like David, you've got to *choose to take action* in the area of passion God has placed inside your heart.

Increasing Your Exposure

I saw this idea play out yet again when I was talking to a Hispanic leader about his area of holy discontent several months ago. He leads a growing multicultural church that is one of the finest ministries I've had the pleasure of being around. During our conversation, I asked him how he wound up leading a church that behaved in such a loving manner across racial lines.

His answer was jarring.

"I grew up in a 'white' church that had no Hispanics in it except for my family," he said. "We felt degraded and devalued every single time we went to church. We were always excluded and subjected to all sorts of unkind remarks.

"It was a palpable hatred," he continued, "and we finally got to a point where my family just couldn't take it anymore. One by one, my parents, my siblings ... they all walked away from that little church, never to return again."

The pastor described how gut-wrenching an experience it had been to be told blatantly who mattered and who didn't at that church ... and then to realize that his family was part of the "who didn't" category. He watched as his dad left the church disillusioned, followed by each of his siblings. "But the day I watched my *mother* leave," he said, "I decided that if it was the last thing I did, I would devote myself to creating a thriving, Acts 2 church that was welcoming of *all* races and cultures."

He lived with that conviction until the day when God gave him the vision to start a multicultural community. I believe that the faithful, passionate leadership he exhibits today is due solely to the fact that he leads from his place of holy discontent which agrees with God that racism in churches is not acceptable.

This pastor knew all too well the realities that existed — even within the four walls of a church, mind you. Instead of caving to them, though, he outclassed them. He let the discrimination that his family had faced fuel his present effectiveness in changing church for the better in his corner of the world.

●

I think the reason I love guys like this who refuse to stand by yawning while congregations veer off-course is because the biggest "giants in my land" on a day-in, day-out basis are local churches that are just plain failing. They've missed the plot altogether and are barely hanging on. *Nothing* wrecks me like this wrecks me!

I attend a struggling church in the little town where I take my summer breaks. In fact, part of my explicit purpose in going is *because* it's struggling. Each week, I sit in the exact same place — aisle seat, third to the last row. And each week, I experience the agony of worshiping in a defeated church.

The awful reality of their plight gets me every time. I know this because after every service I attend with that fifty-person congregation, I drive home with a little firmer grip on the steering wheel, a little more angst in my spirit, and a little more fire in my gut to keep fighting for the health of local churches.

Exposing my heart one more time to the thing that wrecks it only urges me to refresh my personal mission: if it's the last thing I do, I will give every ounce of the rest of my life to helping churches get better. I will keep a serving towel permanently folded over my arm, doing whatever I can so that local churches and their leaders have half a shot at prevailing.

Sure, once I get a little distance from each weekend's pitiful experience, I console myself by considering the endless job security I have because of lifeless churches like this one. There is a lot of work to be done out there! I also take solace in the fact that some churches really *are* prevailing. But think about this with me: if I only allowed myself to worship in places like Willow or North Point or Fellowship or Salem Baptist or dozens of other churches I know, I would think every church on the planet was the picture of health and vitality. No, it's only when I step foot into aimless, uninviting, flat-lined churches that I see my God-given mission has some staying power.

My point? Once you find your holy discontent, do whatever you must do to feed it. Again, if it sounds counterintuitive, it's because it is. But as I've often said, the great ongoing danger regarding a person's holy discontent is that its energy will wane. The fuel will dry up. The firestorm will fizzle out. No matter how amped up we are about something that wrecks us, time and repetition take a toll. Another plate of food for a starving orphan, another late-night music rehearsal for an artist, another tutoring class for an inner-city child—if we aren't diligent to feed our holy discontent, we will assuredly become "weary in well doing,"[1] to borrow a phrase from the apostle Paul.

Determine now that you will never insulate yourself from what wrecks you. Instead, *increase* your exposure ... and then hang on to your hat, because *real* living is going to rock your world when you begin to share space with your holy discontent! Popeye had to get his clothes a little wrinkled and his fingernails a little dirty when acting on whatever it was that he couldn't stand. Most likely, so will you. But one thing is certain: you'll never regret a single moment lived from the energy of your fueled holy discontent.

Don't Give Up

Some of you may be glazed over at this point, thinking, *Bill, I'd be more than happy to feed my discontent ... if only I knew what in the world it was!* If you fall into that category, can I ask you to make a deal with me? Please don't give up. It may take you awhile to discover it, but read this closely: it is *never* too late for you to locate your holy discontent, and it could be that a little experimentation is all you need to get in touch with what you can't stand.

I firmly believe that if you will expand your world; if you will expose yourself to soulful experiences that stretch your thinking; and if you will seize innovative opportunities for service, then *something* in our need-laden world will grab hold of you and just not let go.

Enlarge your world. Travel outside of your normal circuits. Visit other ministries and organizations. Venture into the inner city. Get amongst the poor. Go on a mission trip to places like the ones that sparked something in Bob Pierce or Mother Teresa. Walk into an AIDS clinic or a Habitat for Humanity home. Pick up your phone, call 1.800.HELPNOW and ask the Red Cross volunteer who answers how you can be of service. You just never know where a move like that might lead you!

Eventually, there will come a sight, there will come a sound, that makes you rise up and say, "Now *that*, I cannot stand!" Eventually, the angst inside you will rise to the level that you simply have to do something or you will utterly implode. Eventually, you'll encounter a bush that's on fire, and you'll hear God say, "So good to see you here! I just knew you wouldn't give up! Now, let's have a chat...."

●

Two years ago, my friend Bob Atkins retired from his role as president of a highly successful company. I know from many candid conversations over the course of our friendship that he truly loved the challenges and risks associated with taking an international company to staggering levels of profitability. Ask him what he enjoyed most about his days in corporate America, and he'll tell you that creating high-performance business units and then pulling the absolute best out of their leaders was about the biggest thrill in his life for many, many years. Bob had a fundamental assumption that everyone wanted to be part of a winning team, so he'd go for the gold quarter after quarter, pushing his people toward ever-loftier goals.

Interestingly, unbeknownst to Bob, God was forging something significant in him during all those years as a senior executive. God was preparing him for his perfectly suited mission—a mission that would powerfully leverage both Bob's industry knowledge *and* his team-building skills.

Just days after Hurricane Katrina hit the Gulf Coast region during the summer of 2005, staff members and volunteers from Willow Creek convened in a conference room to come up with a plan of action for providing aid to the people who had been hit hardest by the storm. Although

Bob Atkins wasn't present, Bob's buddy Dave was one of the volunteers in that work session, and one item on the agenda was to brainstorm candidates who might be willing to relocate to Waveland, Mississippi, for nine weeks to help manage the volunteer teams that would be arriving on a regular basis. Dave thought this sounded like the *perfect* role for Bob so he nominated him and told the team he'd call Bob right away to let him know that this group had his immediate-term plans all figured out. (Don't we all love friends like Dave.)

Willow had raised a bunch of money to assist with post-hurricane relief efforts and had arranged for two busloads of volunteers to travel down to the affected areas each week and help feed, clothe, and provide shelter for families who had tragically lost everything. The only missing link was finding someone who was smart with money and who could be a consistent set of eyes and ears to coordinate the massive volunteer effort.

Guess who had a burning-bush conversation with God that day? "It was pretty straight-forward, actually," Bob told me recently. "*You need to step up, Bob. Now!*—That's about all God said."

Bob's Popeye moment happened on the heels of watching the heart-wrenching footage of the hurricane's aftermath every night on the news. He and one of Willow's teaching pastors took an exploratory trip to Waveland to see the devastation firsthand, and it was then that he realized things were much, much worse than he ever imagined. With his Popeye moment energizing him all the way, he headed back home, talked to his wife, prayed to confirm his decision, and then packed his bags.

"A huge need existed, and I kept getting the sense that I was supposed to help meet it," Bob said. "For so long—decades, really—I was perfectly content just to write checks and send them off to various places ... ministries and worthwhile nonprofits. But this time, it was *personal*. This time, I had seen with my own two eyes the horrible quandary entire cities of people were in, and I couldn't stand on the sidelines anymore. They had lost their homes. They had lost their belongings. They had lost their dignity. And for most of them, insurance couldn't begin to touch the desolation that had overwhelmed their lives.

"*Nobody* should have to live like they were living," Bob said quietly. "Suffering like that just shouldn't exist."

●

Bob and other volunteers from Willow devised a plan, and days later, Bob found himself standing in a circus-style tent in a deserted Kmart parking lot in soggy Waveland, Mississippi. He and his teammates had rented generators, they had prepared meals, they had sorted clothes, and they were ready to serve.

Families began streaming in and were immediately escorted through well-organized aisles that were stocked from floor to ceiling with living essentials, such as toothpaste, boxes of crackers, cans of beans, bottled water, and new clothing—all free of charge. "As days went by, we'd run out of various things, such as underwear," Bob explained, "and so we'd stop what we were doing and pray for underwear. Twenty minutes later, as if on cue, a huge Jockey rig would show up, stuffed to capacity with underwear. The driver would say, 'Uh, I'm not sure what you're gonna do with all this, but ...,' and our team would just erupt in laughter. 'We know *exactly* what we're going to do with it!' we'd tell him. 'We've been waiting for you!'"

In many ways, Bob's involvement in Waveland was the most natural next step he could have taken in life. A few years prior, he had read Bob Buford's inspiring book entitled *Half Time* and came away feeling compelled to give himself to something more than turning a profit. Like Buford, he feared he was becoming just a bored, rich guy. Through Willow Creek, he got involved in an initiative called The Storehouse, a place where new building materials are donated by companies that have excess inventory and then provided to low-income families who don't otherwise have the means to replace their leaky faucets and broken appliances. In Bob's words, "It puts the most in the hands of the least."

And he's right. Some of these families wind up with brand new high-end faucets, worth hundreds of bucks a pop, in their modest homes—it's incredible!

Bob and a few buddies formed a little volunteer board for the Chicago Storehouse and dubbed themselves the "Wise Guys." I look at how seriously they take their roles, how carefully they lay out their long-term strategy, how devoted they remain to the cause, and I just shake my head and think, *This is what happens when a bunch of smart, passionate, godly guys link arms and determine to do battle for the kingdom.* You can't beat it!

Last year, the Storehouse learned that a women's shelter in downtown Chicago called Tabitha House was falling apart. More than thirty single, unemployed moms were residing there, and the conditions were beyond hazardous: the kitchen was run down, the bathrooms were falling apart, light fixtures were broken or nonfunctioning, floors were cracked, and wires were exposed. Immediately, the Wise Guys rolled up their sleeves and got to work. When their network of Storehouse staff, volunteers, and donors were done, Tabitha House boasted a kitchen full of state-of-the-art appliances, a TV for the kids' downstairs playroom, and computers for the new study room ... not to mention a complete, floor-to-ceiling structural renovation.

Because of people like Bob who have such unwavering convictions about serving people who are under-resourced, there are five Storehouses in operation today — in addition to the Chicago location, Storehouse staff and volunteers now meet practical needs in Appalachia, West Virginia; inner-city Los Angeles; the Bronx; and as of early 2006, in Waveland, Mississippi.

Let the story of this sixty something who has found more satisfaction in serving than could be found in *ten* high-flying corporate careers inspire you to keep the hunt going for *your* life's holy discontent.

It's *never* too late.

5

A Worthy Fight

Every August, Willow hosts a conference for local church leaders called the Leadership Summit. Teams of folks work for months in advance to assemble speakers representing the best of the best from a broad spectrum of fields— academia, business, the public sector, ministry, and so on. Although keynote talks are delivered from the main stage in Barrington, they are received via satellite broadcast by 130 sites across North America. The idea is that centrally located churches can invite leaders from their communities and from other nearby churches to hone their leadership gifts without necessarily having to travel to Willow Creek to do so.

Now in its twelfth year, its success continues to amaze those of us who have had a hand in putting it on because we remember all too well the knee-jerk reaction that caused the whole thing to emerge.

5

81

In the early nineties I began to notice a trend. In my domestic travels week in and week out, I would encounter pastor after pastor who was crying out for some leadership input. Many of these men and women topped my "most respected" list, and many of them were far more committed to the cause of building healthy local churches than I was. Regardless, they wanted to get even *better* at leading in their various settings but had no practical way to do so. I was an easy target, so they asked for my input.

Their need should have been so simple to meet, but when I went searching for solid resources to suggest to them, I realized there was no single event that was solely focused on the spiritual gift of leadership. Eventually, my exasperation reached fever pitch. In a fit of frustration one day, I invited my associate Jim Mellado, president of the Willow Creek Association, into my office.

It was a Popeye moment to beat all Popeye moments.

"Jimmy, that's all I can stand, and I can't stand any more! I'll come all the way back to Chicago from my summer leave, I will pull some faculty together, and we will teach on the subject of leadership. If five people come, then I will pour my life into five people," I remember telling him.

"I'll do it for no other reason than to alleviate this mounting rage I'm feeling! The only way I know to get rid of it is to settle on a vision that speaks to it somehow, and what God does with it from there is his business. All I know is I just can't live like this anymore! The church will not prevail unless its leaders prevail, and the church's leaders will not prevail unless they can tap into the wisdom of prevailing leaders who have gone before them."

I was ready to hit something, I was so aggravated. But that intense aggravation—along with my decision to move toward it (find it and feed it, right?)—is what ultimately gave birth to the Leadership Summit. After a three-year run within Willow's four walls, we moved to a satellite approach. That was 1998, and more than 5,500 leaders benefited from solid, biblical training and development that year; today, it reaches more than 70,000 leaders in 37 states and Canada. Only God.

Here's the point I want to make: you absolutely cannot back down from pursuing your area of holy discontent just because the risk meter registers high. Despite the fact that I was utterly determined to launch the Summit that first year, I knew I was assuming a *boatload* of risk. As a leadership team, we'd devoted a whole slew of staff and a sizable bundle of money to this project, really having no idea if it would work out. If it flopped, the destructive ripple effect could cripple huge pieces of our ministry for months to come. That being the case, it remained something that just had to get done.

When It Gets Risky, Fight for It

Sometimes, you think you've seen the apex of risk come and go in a given situation, only to be greeted by a challenge that *really* knocks the wind out of you. Although launching Leadership Summit was laden with the potential for enormous peril, riskier still was the decision several years later to take the entire conference abroad.

On a cold night in November of 2004, I sat in a room with other leaders who oversee the activity of the Willow Creek Association, which serves as a nonprofit resource center for more than twelve thousand member churches. I had barely slept the night before this particular board meeting because I knew the conversation on this evening's docket had enormous implications for the foreseeable future, both for the Association and for me. I don't know about you, but these are the moments I live for!

We tackled the other items on the agenda and took a quick break before reconvening for a brainstorming session about investing what would amount to thousands of hours and millions of dollars in hosting a "Global Summit." Something like this had never been done before, and so the first hour of the discussion was jam-packed with questions: Will what works in the States translate to these other cultures and people groups? Is the need for leadership development the same in other countries as it is here in our own back yard? Is the relational currency our leadership team has with our international partners enough to be able to pull this off with excellence?

Executing a Global Summit—and doing it well—would require *massive* amounts of faith and dogged determination from a lot of key staff. Not to mention a few financial stars falling into perfect alignment so that we could commit to this type of event not just once but for many years to come.

•

The following September, by God's grace, the first Global Summit was born. I had traveled overseas to offer an in-person greeting to the primary host site in Norway. Once I'd done my part and settled into a front-row seat to view that first-ever video broadcast, my heart swelled. *This is the undeniable, unquenchable, unstoppable force that only materializes when we fight for our holy discontent!* I thought. I absorbed the teaching that week with humble appreciation for the fact that tens of thousands of pastors and leaders would get better as a result of those Summits, which meant that their churches would also get better.

Nothing could have pleased me more.

When the stakes are higher than they've ever been before ... when the threat of failure looms like a caged animal waiting to pounce ... when the skyrocketing risk level makes you want to lose your lunch ... *that* is when it's a gloves-off fight to the finish for the sake of your holy discontent, friends. When you find it, you've got to feed it. But it's also true that when it gets risky, you simply *must* fight for it.

A Focus on Hope

For the remainder of this chapter I'd like to paint a portrait for you of what it looks like to embrace risk and *fight* for your holy discontent when the smooth seas you're sailing suddenly become turbulent. There's a woman who lives, works, and serves in Detroit who personifies this progression about as well as anyone I know.

I had the privilege of doing a live interview with Eleanor Josaitis during one of the sessions at the 2005 Leadership Summit. Her responses all underscored a belief I've held for as long as I can remember, which is that if something is worth giving your life to, it will inherently involve a high measure of risk. In fact, I don't know *anyone* who has given himself or herself fully to a cause who has not encountered the kind of do-or-die risk that weakens the knees of even the steadiest among us.

A few weeks before Summit rolled around, an associate of mine and I paid a visit to the civil and human rights organization Eleanor cofounded nearly forty years ago. I'd heard about Focus: HOPE throughout the years and was always impressed with their innovative, passionate approach to wiping out racism, poverty, and injustice in Detroit and the surrounding areas.

Their headquarters is situated on forty acres in the heart of Detroit, which as you know is not exactly the safest, most pristine city in America. Homeless people hover beneath overpasses, which are riddled with spray-painted graffiti. Drug deals and violent crime are a reality. Life just looks *hard* as you make your way from the interstate to the side street where the campus sits.

The dingy gray of the inner city seems to disappear, though, as you enter the grounds of Focus: HOPE. If you could see this campus for yourself, it would take your breath away! The building interiors are spotless. The land-scaping is immaculate. Not a spot of graffiti to be found on any surface, anywhere. In all directions, you notice only further evidence of the staff's commitment to excellence and efficiency. The other thing you notice is that Eleanor herself lives, breathes, eats, and bleeds the Focus: HOPE cause.

•

Like most people I come across, Eleanor remembers exactly where she was and what she was doing when her Popeye moment occurred. A suburban Detroit housewife with a husband, five kids, and an otherwise predictable life, Eleanor found herself on the couch on a hot summer's night in 1963 watching a TV special about the historic Nuremburg trials following World War II.

"The thought of people being treated like animals or of being gassed to death was sickening," Eleanor told us that day. She said that as she sat there watching the awful account, she wondered what she would have done if she had lived in Nazi Germany in those days: How would she have responded if she'd seen that level of abuse firsthand?

In her living room that night, the TV broadcast was interrupted by a breaking news report. Eleanor listened closely as reporters said that all hell had burst loose in Birmingham, Alabama, where a civil rights march turned violent.

She watched in horror as police officers gave electric shocks with cattle prods to protestors. Fire hoses were turned on innocent people. "I cried my eyes out," Eleanor said. "All I could think was, *How can this be happening in America?!*"

That evening, a firestorm of frustration so gigantic welled up inside Eleanor that she knew she'd implode if she didn't act on it. "It changed me forever. I immediately became a very strong supporter of Dr. [Martin Luther] King and resolved that I was going to give myself to the exact same cause he was fighting so tirelessly for—racial reconciliation."

We were sitting across from each other in the modest boardroom of Focus: HOPE as she recounted what ensued from there. I could tell she had dozens of competing thoughts whirling around in her mind just waiting to come out. The radical passion this woman had felt almost half a century earlier was still alive and well. What a testimony to the high-voltage living people experience when they find and feed their holy discontent!

She abruptly pushed her chair back, hopped up, and muttered something about showing me exactly what had sparked her Popeye moment, but her voice trailed off as she disappeared. Twenty seconds later, she returned with a hardcover book in hand, *The Civil Rights Movement: A Photographic History*.[1] When she laid it in front of me on the table, the spine cracked open to a page I could tell had been studied many times before.

"Here's what I saw that day on TV," she said. "Look at this—it's atrocious!" She pointed to a photograph of a black demonstrator being mauled by police dogs. Another picture showed two dozen black people sitting on a sidewalk, hands cupped behind their heads, as local firefighters shot water from high-pressure hoses at their backs.

"I'd wondered what I would have done had I lived in *Germany*," she continued. "But that night in front of my TV the question became, 'What am I doing in my *own* country?' Then and there, I decided that some things were going to change for my family and me. Drastically change."

In 1968, after the Detroit riots tore apart her own community, Eleanor and her husband packed up the family's belongings, pulled up stakes from a comfortable suburban home, and relocated themselves to Detroit, risking everything to feed her holy discontent: creature comforts, family solidarity, personal safety, future stability, reputation. According to Eleanor, though, the decision was perfectly logical: "Your goal in life has to be bigger than yourself, Bill. Until that move, mine wasn't."

Twenty-four hours after the Detroit riots ended, Eleanor and a family friend, the late Father William Cunningham, walked the downtown streets and were appalled as they saw the National Guard riding down the boulevard in armed tanks. "We repeated the same question over and over to each other," she said. "What can we do to get these communities to come together?"

Soon after, the two friends set up an office in the basement of Father Cunningham's church just one block from Focus: HOPE's current campus, rallied a few volunteer partners, and began meeting regularly to devise an appropriate strategy for responding to the racial tension in

Detroit. As they dug in, they realized that before they could expect people to hear their plan for racial reconciliation, they needed to silence the much-louder noise that was competing for attention: grumbling stomachs.

Detroit had an insidious hunger problem that first needed to be addressed, so Eleanor and Father Cunningham pointed all their energy in that direction.

Focus: HOPE is the brainchild of two people who refused to stand by and watch racial segregation and pervasive hunger take down their city. These days, their world-renowned food program, which is the largest of its kind in the nation, provides commodity foods for well over a thousand women, children, and senior citizens every day. I was profoundly impacted as we walked through the main distribution center, located in the heart of the campus. Set up just like a supermarket, there are volunteers who welcome under-resourced families, provide carts, hand out shopping lists, and staff check-out lines. They go to all this trouble so that the process of getting groceries at Focus: HOPE can be as dignified as possible for kids who come with their parents to shop. Hopefully, the experience teaches them to lead self-sufficient lifestyles that add value to the economy instead of relying on handouts for the rest of their lives.

Moreover, to reinforce this goal, Focus: HOPE offers state-of-the-art training and education programs so that men and women can get off the food program and begin making a contribution in local industry. So far, Focus: HOPE has graduated more than eight thousand people into jobs with starting salaries that are double the minimum wage.

You can't expose yourself to the progress of Focus: HOPE without appreciating the intelligence behind the organization. A lot of people dream dreams and chase visions but never think through the mechanics, the execution, of how to actually bring the thing to ground. From the day-care program for the children of those who are working and being trained, to the wisdom of enlisting local auto-makers to co-create job training programs, Focus: HOPE possesses sophistication at every level ... and an end result that really does help people create a new life for themselves.

●

During a recent interview with a reporter from a local news agency, Eleanor was reminded of the far-reaching impact of Focus: HOPE's efforts. "The reporter was a professional young woman," Eleanor explained, "and in addition to being a successful journalist, she was just a great people person. At the end of the interview, the reporter gathered her belongings and stood up to leave. Before she got to the door, she turned toward me and said, 'You probably don't know this, Mrs. Josaitis, but I grew up on your food program. I can't leave without saying thank you. This organization saved my family's life.'"

"I get that all the time," Eleanor said with a wide smile, "from the strangest of places."

Making a Difference

Every Tuesday morning Eleanor personally orients new employees (called "colleagues") to the Focus: HOPE culture. She takes them through the history of the organization using a massive file folder she showed me during our meeting. It contains pictures of condemned houses that Focus: HOPE had renovated and rented out to families in need. Newspaper clippings detailing the ribbon-cutting ceremony for Focus: HOPE's machinist training school. Father Cunningham's obituary. Personal letters from people in the community who were either inspired or outraged by Focus: HOPE's work. Copies of paychecks former Focus: HOPE students were now receiving out in the marketplace. Photos of former Focus: HOPE members who had left the organization and then sadly lost the battle to addiction or abuse or violence. "These people didn't have to die," she said. "A little assistance, a little training, one good opportunity to make it in this world … they didn't have to die."

She says that she wants new colleagues—especially younger ones who weren't even alive in 1967—to understand their organization's roots and the risks associated with joining the team. She asks every new colleague, "When was the last time you looked at the world around you and said, '*This* is not acceptable'? When was the last time you sucked up the courage and wrote to your elected officials about a situation that you just won't tolerate anymore?" (Trust me, if Eleanor Josaitis asked you this in person, you'd have pen in hand right now. She's about as feisty as they come.)

"When was the last time you cared enough to check in on your neighbors, your family members, your friends, to make sure they have enough to eat? Look around you! Who needs help but is too proud to ask for it? *That's* where you can shine!"

But it's not just *paid* staff that Eleanor builds into. The organization uses the services of more than fifty thousand volunteers, many of them high profile community and industry leaders. I'd be willing to bet that in many cases, they're probably scratching the itch of their own holy discontent by showing up to help.

When Eleanor and I were making our way to the conference room that morning, I happened to see a nameplate on one desk that read, "Lloyd Reuss."

"Is this *Lloyd Reuss* ... as in the former president of General Motors?"

"Oh, yeah!" Eleanor answered. "GM had him, but now we do. He works here ... for free, that is."

"Heck of a qualified volunteer," I mentioned as we kept walking.

Eleanor isn't an intimidating or especially powerful-looking person. She barely reaches five feet tall, she's well into her seventies, and her disarming charm tilts the ratio more toward grandmother than guerrilla. But she is one of the most passionate risk-takers I've ever met. Because of this, guys like Lloyd Reuss and other high-capacity leaders line right up, ready to do whatever it takes to engage in the fight with her.

•

Later that day, Eleanor stepped out of our meeting to get a cup of coffee, and while she was gone, I paged through the civil rights book she'd brought in earlier. The photos were all in black and white, all terribly disturbing. Page after page of riotous mobs beating men and women with clubs. Malcolm X in front of his firebombed Queens home. Dr. King's sons and daughter peering into the open casket that held their lifeless dad.

The injustice, the destruction, the loss of life—it's all unspeakable, I thought as I sat there. The images of the events that took place right there in Detroit—as well as in Chicago, L.A., and dozens of cities in the South—flashed through my mind as I felt a heavy sorrow settle into my chest.

But the sorrow wasn't there by itself. I also felt an *enormous* sense of anticipation for the future because people like Eleanor exist. Here's a woman who sold her house, uprooted her family to live in the inner city, nearly had her kids taken away by court order, was disowned by a father-in-law who couldn't understand her passion, lost friends, lost family members, and lost respect from scores of onlookers who thought she'd absolutely flipped out (she's got the hate mail to prove it) ... all for the sake of a worthy cause.

Then, when that amount of risk just wasn't enough, she boarded a plane for Washington, DC, to testify before the

House and Senate no fewer than thirty-two times to request additional federal aid for the people she was trying to serve in Detroit.

She's still fighting for those dollars today.

●

Can I shoot straight here? I don't own a crystal ball. I don't have an "in" with God where he tells me what he's going to unfold in the days to come. I don't know how much worse the circumstances surrounding us will become before things start to turn around. But this much I do know: the world is a much richer place because of bold, fearless risk-takers like Eleanor Josaitis who find their holy discontent and then feed it, who lean into it even when it gets tough, and who work tirelessly to make tomorrow better than today.

Peace, Love, and Peanut Butter

A few minutes after she'd excused herself, Eleanor stepped back into the meeting room, coffee in hand. Unprompted, she said, "You know, forty-five years ago, the only options for women were essentially teaching and nursing. I wanted to be a nurse, but everyone told me my personality wouldn't fit with that profession. I was devastated ... really, just *devastated*."

Evidently, it took Eleanor a long time to get over that heartbreak, but in the end it was probably that dead end that allowed her instead to take the path leading to Focus: HOPE. "Now as I look back on it all, I realize that *success* was never my goal," she continued. "I didn't want to be a nurse so that I'd be 'successful.' I wanted to be a nurse because it was the most effective way I knew to get results and to change lives!"

I'd say she's done both after all.

●

Frequently, Focus: HOPE hosts third graders both from the inner city and from the suburbs at their downtown facility. Eleanor and her team stick dozens of these eight-year-olds in the same room so they can rub elbows and share stories and begin to see life from the other one's perspective.

Just before my associate and I left to catch our flight back to Chicago, Eleanor flipped toward the back of her bulging file folder and pulled out a photo. The picture had been taken some months prior and showed a few white kids and a few black kids, all hovered around her. Everyone had huge smiles on their faces and silver spoons in their hands. Eleanor beamed as she explained its significance.

"Last time the kids were here, I overheard one of them—a white kid from the burbs—chattering away to a black boy whose family lives in the inner city. With all the enthusiasm an eight-year-old can muster, he said, '*You* like peanut butter?! Well, *I* like peanut butter too! We're both the same!'

"I stood over those two precious kids who were sitting cross-legged on the floor that afternoon," Eleanor continued, "and thought, *Maybe it doesn't have to be so difficult after all.*"

Friends, only a true Popeye person can embrace the level of risk Eleanor has embraced and come away believing that the task isn't too big to accomplish, the road isn't too long to keep walking, and the obstacles really aren't too high to continue fighting. Like I said previously, anything worth pursuing is going to require *great* risk.

I wonder, are you risking enough for *your* holy discontent?

6

Wherever It Takes You, Whenever It Takes You There

Ready for the third consideration as it relates to managing your holy discontent? As you'll recall, once you find it, the wisest thing you can do is to *feed* it. Next, when things get risky, as they are sure to do, you've got to dig in and summon the necessary resources to *fight* for it. But equally important is this: if your holy discontent decides somewhere along the line to morph, my advice to you is to *follow* it.

One of the best examples of this concept is found in the life of an Old Testament guy named Nehemiah. His story opens up with him kicked back in a life of luxury inside the splendor of a Persian palace—Nehemiah had the cushy job of cupbearer, the person responsible for taste-testing the king's wine just to be sure nobody had lost his better

99

judgment and had tried to poison him. I guess you could say that death loomed on a daily basis for a cupbearer, but there were certainly tougher jobs to be had.

One day Nehemiah received some unexpected and up-setting news from his ancestral home of Jerusalem. His brother and some of his buddies had just returned from paying Jerusalem a visit, and their report was totally de-moralizing. "The 'conditions are *appalling,*'" they told him. "'The wall of Jerusalem is still rubble, the city gates are still cinders.'"[1] Nehemiah was told that his fellow Jews—those who had survived the exile, at least—were in bad shape;[2] because their wall of protection no longer existed, they were vulnerable to attack from robber bands. Moreover, surrounding nations were ridiculing the God who wasn't even strong enough to protect his own people ... or so it seemed.

Little did they know, this "impotent" God had a *very* powerful plan in mind.

•

From Nehemiah's perspective, the broken-down walls weren't nearly as big an issue as the fact that neighboring countries were laughing out loud at the "powerless God" of the Israelites. He knew that if the city's wall weren't rebuilt—and soon—his fellow people would be assimilated into other cultures and would most likely lose their iden-tity and their religion. He couldn't stand for that! So what did he do? Well, like any leader worth his salt, Nehemiah the Great sat down and had a good cry.

It's true. The situation was so devastating to him that he just broke down bawling like a baby. Nehemiah was facing his own Popeye moment—that's all he could stand, and he couldn't stand any more. In fact, I think it was just raw holy discontent pouring out of the guy as he lay on the ground heaving wet sobs. Being the activist that he was, though, Nehemiah couldn't stay face-down for long. His mourning, fasting, and prayer[3] turned quickly to action as he hopped up, resigned from his Persian post, and got busy solving the problem that faced him. Risking life and limb—as well as his reputation—Nehemiah asked a foreign king for safe passage and provisions to go tackle the task he knew had his name all over it. If rebuilding a wall would get the mocking of his God to cease, then rebuilding a wall was exactly what he would do!

●

Like Nehemiah, sometimes you'll get partway through your life believing that your purpose, your identity, and your mission are all tied up in one thing, only to realize that at some point along the way, that "one thing" morphed on you. Don't forget, Nehemiah had a great gig before his famed wall-building season. Nehemiah the Cupbearer— the most influential, noted, and prestigious servant of the king … it's how *everyone* knew him. And he was going to throw it all away just because of a few loose bricks and a gate that was ajar?

God was calling Nehemiah to participate in a "new thing." Interestingly, it just so happened that this new thing would require solid leadership acumen, fantastic communication capability, and unflinching tenacity—all skills Nehemiah had honed during his palace days.

What first got him in the game was an isolated incident that he just couldn't *stand*. But what kept Nehemiah motivated for fifty-two solid days, energized to fend off mounting criticism as he and his associates accomplished the good work of rebuilding the great wall of Jerusalem, was a *new holy discontent*—a gut-deep belief that the name of God should be honored and the people of God should be protected. In the end, Nehemiah led one of the most impressive reconstruction efforts in all of recorded history.

The Evolution of Discontent

Friends, this "new thing" dynamic isn't reserved for ancient leaders with unusual names and a penchant for the construction business. Once you know what you're looking for, you'll find that modern-day examples are everywhere.

About twenty years ago something snapped inside the lead singer of the Irish group U2. Bono and his band had played at a day-long "Live Aid" concert that was put on to raise money for Ethiopian famine victims. The event was held at Wembley Stadium in London but another 1.5 billion fans in a hundred countries watched it via video broadcast—it ended up being a profoundly moving experience for *everyone* involved ... but especially for Bono.

Soon after that event he and his wife, Ali, boarded a flight headed for the Horn of Africa to see for themselves the tumult that was taking place. They hadn't told anyone they were going. It was something they did quietly, privately, just so Bono could get the images of "those starving people he was seeing on television"[4] out of his mind. Bono would spend a good portion of that summer working at an Ethiopian feeding camp and would never be the same again.

●

Fast-forward to today, and you'll find Bono using his unprecedented fame and influence to draw attention to this generation's most pressing issues, extreme poverty, of course, being one of them. Bono has lobbied powerful world leaders for the cancellation of the debt that plagues two-thirds of the world. He's fought tooth and nail for funding to fight the AIDS pandemic. He works diligently to reform trade policy. (All of this in addition to fulfilling some pretty intense rock star obligations. You thought *your* plate was full.)

During U2's most recent tour Bono made provisions for my family and several of our friends to attend one of the band's performances when they came through Chicago. Near the end of the concert as the raucous crowd was begging for more, he stopped everything and yelled out at his fans, "Are you ready to save the world?!" Everyone screamed and cheered, having no idea where all of this was going.

"Lift up your cell phones," Bono shouted, "and text your name to the number on the screen ... now!" Right then, the screens lighted up with the digits of a phone number. "Your message is going to One: The Campaign to Make Poverty History. You will be joining more than 1.6 million Americans who have already chosen to get involved in eradicating extreme poverty all over the world ... something that's going to happen in our generation, if I have anything to say about it."[5]

Instantaneously, lighted cell-phone screens dotted the dark auditorium as tens of thousands of people text-messaged their support. During the very next song, using technological savvy I'll never fully grasp, the names of people in that Chicago venue who had joined the campaign flashed across the giant image magnification screens behind the band. People went nuts as they saw their names appear.

Following that fantastic experience, I was struck by two things. The first is that the innumerable complaints I've received over the decades from people who gripe that the worship music at Willow is too loud are *completely* unjustified. Until they've been to a U2 concert and have gone home with ears bleeding, I don't want to hear another word from them. (Actually, for three solid days following the concert, I couldn't have heard them anyway. Ringing ... that's all that existed in my auditory universe. Ringing and a dull, throbbing brain-ache. Best pain I've ever known.)

The second (and far more substantial) take-away was just how devoted Bono is to his holy discontent. If I had to classify it, I'd call his cause *dismantling apathy*. He just can't *stand* apathy! If you've been to a U2 concert, then you know exactly what I'm talking about. The guy *hates* passionless singing. He won't tolerate half-hearted songwriting. Lifeless performances make him crazy! It stands to reason, then, that he would wage all-out war against apathy on other fronts. His battle cry in the fight against the injustices plaguing our world is clear: "Think that because you're rich, you can ignore the poor? Think that since you're healthy you can just leave the diseased to die? Not on my watch!"

Each time I catch sight of Bono's latest efforts, I have to remind myself that this is the same person who has money to burn and all the fame a person could ever want or need in a lifetime ... or twenty, for that matter. It's the same Bono who has sold more than 130 million albums, the same Bono who has played dozens of sold-out world tours, and the same Bono whose flashy image has made him one of the most recognizable cultural icons of the modern age. He's altogether the same. And yet he's completely *different*. Why? Because his holy discontent morphed, and he chose to follow it. He was so stirred up in his soul after serving the poor in Ethiopia that he finally said, "I've got to give myself to something more than making records."

●

Just a few weeks after that Chicago concert, Bono spoke at the National Prayer Breakfast here in the United States. He stood up in front of heads of state and foreign dignitaries and challenged them to do more than they were already doing because, according to Bono, "when the history books are written, our age will be remembered for three things: the war on terror, the digital revolution, and what we did—or did not to—to put the fire out in Africa."[6]

My point is that everywhere Bono goes, his cause *oozes* out of him. I actually remember when this realization first hit me. I was in Dublin to train pastors, and since Bono knew I was in town, he invited me to drop by a recording session the band was doing for a new CD. I spent several hours at the studio that night, splitting time between watching the guys complete one track after another and catching up with Bono.

We'd start talking about debt relief for certain countries, and Bono would get all fired up. We'd migrate to the topic of personal faith, and he'd fire up even more. We'd hit AIDS, and he'd just about come undone. In between passionate spiels, he would grab his guitar and start playing a new song he was testing out that related to the topic at hand. It was the most powerful fusion of a person's holy discontent and sheer art that I have ever witnessed.

You can't spend time with Bono without detecting his *incredible* energy for life—an inner vitality that I liken to a bright, bright bulb. Most household light bulbs come in 25-watt or 75-watt or 100-watt varieties, but I'm convinced that Bono is running constantly at about a thousand.

Frankly, I always come away from encounters with him just shaking my head in disbelief. Since his childhood days all Bono wanted to be was a rock star. Today he's one of the leading proponents for eradicating extreme poverty in the world. And you can trace this all back to the morphing of his holy discontent, which forced him to stare into the eyes of starving children in Addis Ababa, Ethiopia, who didn't even have the energy to stand up to greet him. Bono's simple response to that experience rekindled the firestorm that was deep in his soul: "I will *not* be in a world where [this reality] continues to be true."[7]

Perhaps God is inviting you into a new-thing dynamic right now. Whatever it is, will you attack it with reckless abandon, giving it your *thousand-watt* all? If you're called at this stage of the game to be a leader, then be a thousand-watt leader! If you're called to be a singer, then be a thousand-watt singer! Fill in the blank with whatever it may be for you—a pilot, an executive, a mom, a dad, a prayer warrior. I *dare* you to approach your holy discontent with an upfront commitment of being "thousand-watt" at whatever you do.

The Next Evolution for Me

Believe it or not, Bono and I have something in common. I know you'll be shocked to discover it's not our singing ability. Or the sunglasses collection. It's something I've come to consider the *next evolution* of the holy discontent God started growing in me when I was just a kid, as I explained in chapter 3.

Although I've always been passionate about helping local churches and local church leaders win, increasingly, I have sensed God calling me into an intense era of focused attention on those who are under-resourced in our world. I sense him asking me to apply the things that I've learned in thirty-plus years of local church ministry to the needs of a much broader community.

About seven years ago, a Willow Creek Association staff member invited me to cross an ocean with him and serve in a country saddled with problems that seemingly had no solutions. The trip opened me up in ways that would radically change the course of my life from that point forward. I hadn't yet developed language around the find-it-feed-it idea, but intuitively, that's exactly what I did over the months and years that followed. I wrenched my already-taxed schedule completely out of whack in order to expose myself to more international realities. I signed up for speaking engagements in some of the hardest parts of the world when I didn't have to—just to see what God was trying to unfold in my life. I read everything I could get my hands on about the struggles of people in tough places like South Africa, Zambia, Namibia, Brazil, Ecuador, Russia, and Ukraine.

Every time I boarded a plane to return home, I realized that my heart had been wrecked just a little bit more from what I had seen on that particular trip—in a good way, of course. In my private times with God, I consistently was drawn closer to his heart for the under-resourced. Passages like the one in James where he says that the only "religion that God our Father accepts as pure and faultless is this: to look after orphans and widows in their distress"[8] convicted me at a deep, deep level. I had to ask, "Am I really doing all that I can do in this arena, given the platform that God has blessed me with?"

In my heart, I knew the answer was no.

For the first time in a long time, I was required to stop all of the worthy, kingdom-building things I was doing and take a look inside myself. Here's the question I sought — and am still seeking — to answer: "What do the poverty issues, the AIDS issues, the justice issues in our world demand of someone like me with the influence God graciously has given me?"

This is an important question to answer because as a pastor, I believe my primary job is to teach what the Bible says about the great issues of the day. Not just *some* of the issues, but *all* of them. The number of times Scripture mentions God's passionate concern for the poor, the oppressed, the widows, the orphans, those who are incarcerated, and those who have no voice is astounding!

I'm realizing more and more that *these* are the "injustices" that the Bible speaks to with greatest power and frequency, and so these are the issues I'm wrestling with. Am I doing ... and are *we* doing ... a good enough job collectively as believers to raise the consciousness levels of people in our community about the justice issues in the Bible that God spent *a lot* of time underlining? How do we respond with the love and grace and relational intelligence of the One whose name we bear ... and yet not back down from the fights that must be fought? Then, even more importantly, what do we do about them? Do we march? Do we write letters? Do we run for office? How do we overturn the systems that continue a form of oppression that the Bible speaks strongly against?

Obviously, the first step in answering some of these questions is getting educated on the issues themselves. Take racial discrimination as an example: 2006 marked the second consecutive time that leaders of Salem Baptist Church of Chicago and Willow Creek experienced something called the "Justice Journey." It's essentially a weeklong bus tour to major sites of the civil rights movement—places all throughout Birmingham, Selma, and Memphis, for instance.

The group itself is a microcosm of the reconciliation they're hoping to usher in: the fifty or so travelers are from separate worlds—they hail from two congregations, one black and one primarily white—but are united in their desire to understand racism and its ongoing impact on our society.

One of the Willow folks who helped out with the team's photography needs is a woman named Kathy. We talked recently about what motivates her to stay plugged into the Justice Journey effort when life for her is already jam packed. She's a consultant with a busy job. She has family obligations. She has ongoing volunteer commitments to help Willow create training programs and so on. Why add one more ball to the juggling act—especially when it deals with something as daunting as fighting for racial reconciliation?

"It's true, she said. "This particular issue is really overwhelming because we're trying to counter the effects of the past four hundred years of history. It can be hugely discouraging when you look at it that way! In my view, the better response to the challenge is to ask, *What can we do now to make a difference?*

"It's easy to go into something like this with a skeptical spirit," Kathy went on, "but once you see minds open, hearts change, paradigms shift, and mutual understanding unfold right before your eyes, you gain new energy for staying the course. When you have as deep a desire as I do to see things change, you just have to show up. Your soul doesn't give you a choice in the matter! Ultimately, you have no idea what the end results of your labor will be; all you know is that it's critical that you engage. Each time I show up for a Justice Journey, I know that at a minimum, my presence makes a difference for the other fifty people sitting on the bus, just as their presence makes a difference for me. Beyond that, only God knows where all of this will lead."

●

During last year's Justice Journey, the senior pastor from Salem and I had the opportunity to meet up with the team just as they were about to cross Alabama's infamous

Edmund Pettus Bridge. It's the site of the "Bloody Sunday" conflict, where peaceful civil rights demonstrators were attacked by armed officers who denied them safe passage across the bridge. We led the team in a prayer and then silently walked all the way to the other side.

As I reflected on the experience that night, I thought, *You know, that twenty-minute walk didn't change the world. It didn't erase history or alter the broader public's paradigm about race relations. It received little media attention, passed no new laws, and established no new norms regarding the need to treat people—regardless of skin color—equitably.*

What it *did* do, though, is change every single person who walked. For me personally, I was reminded that *any* step taken toward the "new things" God wants to do in your midst—be it expanding your knowledge, increasing your understanding, or challenging your assumptions—is a meaningful and crucial step.

Taking Hold of Your New Thing

The questions surrounding my morphed holy discontent still outnumber the answers, but this much is crystal clear: I have had quite a ride during my first thirty years of ministry—I've faced some amazing challenges, I've learned tons of lessons, I've had the privilege of partnering with fantastic people, and I've received inconceivable blessings from the same God who gave me this career path in the first place.

Regardless what the next thirty years will hold, I know that I want to be a Moses-type of person who slows down long enough to notice when a bush is on fire right in front of my toes. Like Mother Teresa, I want to hold my plans loosely so that opportune gear shifts or direction changes aren't lost on me. I want to have Bob Pierce's impressive responsiveness so that when God says it's time, I'm ready to rally my resources for the cause. Like dozens of courageous men and women from Willow and from Salem Baptist, I want to increase my exposure and trust God with the results of what I find there. I want to be the type of person who hits optimum impact during the final third of his life and is willing to follow a holy discontent with reckless abandon when it morphs into some new and unexpected challenge.

And like Bono, I want to be a thousand-watt guy whose inner vitality, fundamental calling, and areas of holy discontent merge together to help change the world.

I hope you'll ask the tough questions of your passion pursuits. I hope you'll let God expand and stretch you so that you can participate in whatever "new thing" he wants to do through you. I hope you'll follow your holy discontent wherever it takes you, whenever it takes you there, so that our world—and, more specifically, our churches—can benefit from your wattage in this generation.

Part III

Fanning the Flame —

The Key to Keeping Your Holy Discontent Alive

7

Magnetic Living

About the time I was fleshing out my thoughts around the *holy discontent* concept, I came across a book written by University of Michigan business school professor Robert Quinn. It contained a theory that really resonated with me—something he called the "fundamental state" theory. Essentially, it says that when a person is gripped by a powerful passion (or driven by a holy discontent, you might say), he or she literally enters into a *completely different state of mind*; in fact, they shift mental gears altogether and begin operating on an entirely new level.

According to Quinn, people can actually migrate *at will* from what he calls the "normal state" to a place known as the "fundamental state." This is helpful to know, especially since you may be stuck in the "normal state" without even knowing it. Here's how to tell: in the normal state, you're almost entirely self-absorbed. You have a reactive approach

7

to life. And you try to maintain the status quo, regardless how unbearable the status quo is. Professor Quinn puts it this way in his book, *Building the Bridge as You Walk On It*: "When we accept the world as it is [by living in the normal state], we deny our ability to see something better, and hence our ability to *be* something better. We become what we behold."[1]

Accepting the world as it is.
Denying our ability to see something better.
Denying our ability to *be* something better.

This is life in the *normal state*.
What's *not* normal, Professor Quinn says, is embracing the fact that another state exists.

●

"To remain in the normal state is ultimately to choose slow death,"[2] asserts Quinn. The normal state is so self-seeking that you can spin your wheels for a lifetime and never once impact the world around you. In the *fundamental* state, however, people care so much about getting results that they begin to move and breathe in a totally different realm. They operate with intentionality. They act with *massive* doses of enthusiasm and persistence. They surrender their ego because the cause simply can't afford their pride. They open themselves up to any and all new ideas and forms of input—regardless where those suggestions come from.

People who operate in a "fundamental" state of mind concentrate at higher levels and focus more intensely because the goal they're pursuing *demands* it. They take risks they wouldn't normally take ... because they have to— there's too much at stake not to! Their creativity kicks up a notch. Their energy soars. Their passion swells.

More than a Theory

As I was pulling together my notes to write this manuscript, Bob Quinn agreed to meet in person to talk about some of these ideas. At the tail end of the discussion, he offered up an intriguing example of what it looks like to exist in this "fundamental state," straight from the pages of his own life.

Bob and his wife had recently received a phone call from several leaders at their church who wanted to know if the Quinns would be willing to think and pray about a potential relocation to Australia. It would only be for three years, they explained ... just long enough for Bob to head up the launch of a new ministry initiative the church wanted to plant there. The elders themselves had "prayed fervently" about it and felt confident that God was leading them in the Quinns' direction.

I could only imagine the flood of thoughts that must have gone through his head in the moments that followed. The move would require leaving a stable career that included tenure at one of the most prestigious business schools in the world; leaving proximity to children and grandchildren; leaving the secure future he'd worked so hard to build; leaving a tremendous circle of supportive friends; leaving exciting challenges in his consulting, training, and writing practices; leaving a great house in the quaint town of Ann Arbor, Michigan ... the works!

When I asked how he felt when he hung up the phone that day, he just grinned and said, "Terrified."

I suppose I should mention here that Bob has a burning, churning holy discontent of his own which revolves around helping people realize their full potential; he just can't *stand* wasted potential! The Australian adventure would afford him incredible opportunities to recruit, build, and sustain a high caliber team of staff and volunteers. Now it would all come down to whether or not he could pry himself away from those "adorable grandkids who have me wrapped around their fingers."

Bob and his wife talked and prayed for a few days before showing up for a meeting the following week with the elders. Mixed with the overwhelming sense of upheaval they were feeling, there was also an indescribable peace that flooded the room as soon as they walked in. "That was the confirmation we both needed to know that this was *exactly* the right thing for us to do," he said. "In that moment—in the space of us yielding to this risky role and saying yes in our hearts—not only did *we* change, but the entire universe *around us* changed. I can't really answer how; I can only tell you that something dramatic happened right then that instantaneously prepared us for the road ahead."

This is a man who doesn't just sit around theorizing ... he actually lives this stuff out. So much so that in the summer of 2006, he and his wife boarded a Qantas flight headed for the Land Down Under with huge hopes for changing lots of lives and making a difference for good in the world. The "fundamental state" had invited him to take a risk he otherwise wouldn't have taken. But it was that powerful drive to *see* something better—and to *be* something better—which thrust him into the game.

You may want to take note: this is what chasing your holy discontent with all you've got can do to you. In the blink of an eye, it's very possible that you too will wake up one day and find yourself relocated to a place I've started calling life's "lunatic fringe," and the only thing crazier than the destination itself is how much you enjoy it once you've arrived.

Better than the Best Day

Bob's story got me thinking about another person I consider to be well-acquainted with the lunatic fringe. I first crossed paths with Jude Goatley several years ago when my wife, Lynne, and I were getting involved with trying to alleviate the AIDS pandemic in Africa. Jude is a New Zealander but now spends the better part of her year serving in a remote village in sub-Saharan Africa.

In the village of Samfya, Jude is what I would call the "relational glue." Her intimate knowledge of the villagers, her radical acceptance of all types of people, her strong interpersonal intelligence, and her disarming style are unequaled.

Jude hadn't always planned on being a missionary in Africa—most career accountants don't. But a trip she had taken as a teenager to visit relatives who were missionaries in Central America served as a Popeye moment where she experienced the wonderful collision of two realities: evidently, there were a lot of kids in the world who needed to be loved, and interestingly enough, she had a huge capacity for loving kids. The impact of that moment would play a huge role in Jude's future. Although she didn't see how playing with kids in central Africa had anything to do with her dedicated financial training, from that day forward, she was sold on international missions in the developing world.

●

The next ten years were an agonizing decade as Jude found herself serving *not* in international missions but rather in corporate accountancy. Despite what the world would consider a very successful career, she acknowledges that for a whole host of reasons, it was the most intense period of confusion and disappointment she'd ever known. But still she persevered (her growing holy discontent demanded it!) and resurfaced after that difficult season just in time to be introduced through a friend of a friend of a friend to an American gentleman from a group called Bright Hope International.

The Palatine, Illinois-based ministry was doing project work in a small village in central Zambia and needed a finance manager on the ground to oversee their food program and to develop their indigenous church-based partnerships. An impossibly high number of people there were dying from diseases—diseases that were either preventable or at least treatable. The figures were sobering: more than a quarter of the people in this community had HIV/AIDS, and because of so many adults dying, more than a thousand children were left orphaned ... representing a staggering 10 percent of the total population in that immediate area. The key was for Bright Hope to find someone who had a compassionate heart for love-starved children and an accounting savvy that was second to none.

You probably know where this story is going.

I don't know about you, but I view an opportunity like that as a wide open door into the "fundamental state." Part of what actually *defines* that state, if you'll recall, is the tendency for people to open themselves up to any and all new ideas and forms of input—regardless where those suggestions come from.

After years and years of waiting, God finally provided an outlet for Jude's holy discontent to get fed; as a result, if you hopped a flight to central Africa today, you'd find Jude joyfully coaching and training leaders in the finer details of project management, budgeting, and bookkeeping. With a whole mob of kids—most of them AIDS orphans— hovering nearby to catch her spare hugs, of course.

The moral of the story is that a bad day lived from the energy of your holy discontent is *far* better than the best day lived anywhere else. I'm sure Jude would agree, despite the fact that the long-awaited "new thing" God is doing in her life is far from a cakewalk. In her day-to-day world, disease lurks around every corner. Desperation threatens to envelop her at every turn. Resources are bare. Modern conveniences are nowhere to be found. The needs are overwhelming, the odds are stacked against her, and in her more rational moments, her conscience begs her to just pack it up and head home.

Recently she came down with the fourth bout of malaria she has had in three years. People who endure successive runs of malaria are kind of like pro football players who get sidelined after multiple concussions. You can suit up and try to play your "A" game, but it just doesn't happen; the toll on your body has been far too severe. Coming to this realization one day, Jude finally agreed to take a short break from her work, head to the nearest town to get her hands on some decent medications, and recuperate for a while.

After playing the role of good patient for three weeks, Jude was antsy to get back to Samfya. One afternoon, still riddled with the awful after-effects of malaria—fever, nausea, light-headedness, fatigue—she boarded a commuter flight headed back to her home away from home. Can you imagine how difficult those steps onto the aircraft must have been for her? *My family thinks I'm nuts*, she must have thought. *My friends think I've long-since lost my mind. Why put myself through all of this? Why not settle down, get married, raise a few kids, and just take it easy for a while?*

That would have been a terrific plan, I suppose, except for the fact that Jude had this annoying little firestorm of frustration churning in her gut that even malaria couldn't squelch. Contrary to the popular opinion of those who are mere onlookers to the plight of Samfyans, she truly believes that those villagers have a right to be trained and developed and cared for. They have a right to be fed and clothed and put through school so they can have half a chance at a future and a hope. They have a right to be loved and shown compassion. They have a right to be embraced and not abandoned. And even if it kills her, she will fight until that dying day to ensure that these things become reality.

"Speak up for those who cannot speak for themselves," Jude tells herself, quoting from Proverbs. "Defend the rights of the poor and needy, uphold the rights of the oppressed and the destitute, and rescue the poor and the helpless."[3] These are the reminders that help her gear up for one more day in the dusty, desolate village that to her is nothing short of paradise.

Drawing Others In

Friends, once you see a little progress was made in your area of holy discontent, you'll gladly head back to your "Samfya" too. Why? Because this type of progress is addicting! When you work late into the night to enact change and then finally see things around you shift even two degrees, you'll be as good as hooked too.

You'll make bigger and bigger sacrifices, all for the sake of the cause.

You'll wrench your schedule out of whack, just to stay the course.

You'll fight for all you're worth to ensure that at least *one* person is paying attention to the need.

But that's not all. Because when you step into the fundamental state, not only will *you* change "states," but you will *draw others* into that new state too. Think about this for a moment: when you spend time in the fundamental state, you become an *increasingly attractive* person. After all, who *doesn't* want to hang out with someone who lives passionately, who loves fearlessly, and who embraces risk-laden change?

When you take the tension of *your* holy discontent that's been welling up in you for weeks or months or decades and leverage it for good in the lives of the people you love—engaging friends, family members, and teammates on a much deeper level than they've known by helping them get connected to *their* passion pursuits—you experience a buzz that you'll never want to end, a marvelous dynamic I call *magnetic living*.

The converse, however, is also true. If you are full of darkness and despair, then the only type of "magnetic living" you will be doing is the kind that sucks people into your black hole of despondency. And team-building exercises don't work so well in a room that's pitch black.

Choose now to be the one who is so passionate about seeing results in your area of holy discontent that you literally catapult people to a new level of thinking, a new level of learning, and a new level of living. In short, be the one who invites people to come with you into the fundamental state.

●

I had the opportunity awhile back to chair a meeting that brought together government leaders, business leaders, church leaders, and parachurch ministry leaders—all who are passionate about alleviating the AIDS pandemic in Africa. The question I asked these top leaders to focus attention on was, *What might we accomplish together that none of us could achieve if we all continued to revolve in our separate orbits?*

What fascinated me from a leadership perspective was that the shared holy discontent that emerged around that table was so high—we all desperately wanted to find solutions that would relieve the suffering of people with AIDS—that every *one* of us began drawing the others into the fundamental state, that "altered" state of mind Quinn writes about. Although I didn't have the language yet to name it, I loved what I saw!

Here was a roomful of what I consider "big-dog" leaders—presidents and CEOs and executive directors of this or that—and yet there was not one ounce of grandstanding or turf protection. There was no politicking. No subtle potshots fired at each other. No ego-driven speeches. Instead, everyone listened intently, everyone thought creatively, and everyone was willing to take *massive* risks to achieve the goal.

Throughout our entire session, people were far less focused on what they *wanted* than they were focused on the *results they wanted to create*. Let me say that again: part of what it means to operate in the fundamental state is that you care more about the results you want to create than about getting what you want. This is a critical point in understanding what makes a fundamental-state citizen tick. What was so inspiring to me about that work session was that I saw something I don't have an opportunity to see very often: I was a firsthand witness to proven, powerful leaders leading at the absolute *highest level possible*. What a rush!

At its core, I think this fundamental state idea says that when you mix a soul-stirring passion with a very real sense of urgency, you *ennoble* your personal leadership capability. You expand the boundaries that contain "what's possible." And you invite lots of others to do the same! Obviously, though, we can't live in the fundamental state *all* the time. We have to eat. We have to sleep. We have to pay bills and take out the garbage. Every once in a while, we have to pull in for a pit stop and take time to refuel. But what we can do is to train our minds and our emotions to visit that "fundamental" place—the place where the flame of our holy discontent burns the brightest—with greater and greater frequency.

Results We Create

After the AIDS meeting, I boarded a plane headed for Chicago. As I relaxed against the headrest, still basking in the joy of seeing an entire group of men and women choose the fundamental state over the normal state, I couldn't help but dream about what might happen if the trend spread. You know, what if pastors and businesswomen and local church leaders and teachers and civil servants and Red Cross volunteers all over the globe were so in touch with their holy discontent and were so driven by the passion to get God-honoring results that they all chose to do the same thing consistently, persistently ... expectantly, even?

Just imagine if pastors and other leaders let go of pride, fear, the need to please, and the need to control! What would happen if we took greater risks rather than staying married to the status quo? Or if all of us invited our colleagues and teams to engage on a consistent basis in purpose-finding instead of problem-solving ... asking not *"What do we want?"* but rather *"What results do we want to create?"*

What if leaders and teams joined hands and got on the same page so that trust could accelerate, accountability could increase, blaming could disappear, and learning through trial and error could actually be acceptable behavior?

What if church leaders of every temperament and background and denominational persuasion were *wide open* to the promptings of the Holy Spirit and said, "God, we want your mind on the decisions in front of us, and we already say yes to whatever it is you'd have us do!"

Friends, can you imagine what might happen in corporations and churches and families all over the world if we all got serious about becoming fundamental-state people? I'm just naive enough to believe that it's possible. I believe we can all get better at seeing what ought to be and then working like crazy to actualize it.

As you can tell by now, I believe the fundamental state is a real place. Moreover, I believe that the fundamental state is where the white-hot inner flame of your holy discontent is hiding! Boundaries get expanded there. Leadership competencies get ennobled there. Fear gets stamped out there. Insecurities get upended there. Passion pursuits get clarified there. And depression is asked to take the slow boat home.

If it's up to us to decide how often we'll enter the fundamental state, then let's agree together to frequent it more and more so that the hope God has asked us to spread to this broken world does not die before we get there. Deal?

Hope's Purpose

As I've observed people living out their holy discontent in the last few years, one thing that has baffled me is how many of them didn't commit to their passion pursuits for just a few weeks or months but in some cases for *decades* on end. They've kept going and going and going, never seeming to tire of fighting for whatever cause has them gripped.

Here's a perfect example of what I'm talking about: recently, I was invited to participate in a worship service at a church where the same person has served as senior pastor for fifty years. *Fifty* years!

He got up to give his portion of the talk, and within about three minutes of his starting statement, his voice was escalating, his arms were flailing, his forehead was beading up with sweat—I thought the guy was going to blow a gasket. And this, again, is after doing talks just like this one for five decades. I would have thought the system would be grinding him down by now, but no way! He's still as fired up as ever ... and as *committed* as ever to seeing people pointed to faith in God.

Similarly, I would expect to find people who work a lot with the poor getting wrecked by working in the deplorable conditions that poor people live in. Surely over time they'd become downcast and dismayed ... surely they'd lose focus and lose heart.

I would expect to find people who are trying to solve the complex AIDS dilemma getting utterly overwhelmed.

I would expect to find people who are trying to build churches and help people come to God but who see that the figures are all going the wrong way getting dispirited or wanting to throw in the towel altogether.

My point is that, faced with such crushing realities, wouldn't it stand to reason that holy-discontent-type people would see no recourse other than to succumb to the desperation that inevitably shows up when you spend so much time and energy fighting an uphill battle?

The Greater One in You

First John 4:4 says that for the Christ-follower, "the one who is in you is greater than the one who is in the world." It's because of this truth that, regardless what happens to you throughout the course of your journey, you don't have to allow the unfinished task, the size of the hill, or the depth of society's ills to get you down. If you still believe that with God all things really *are* possible, you owe it to yourself and to the people in your sphere of influence to determine each and every day to keep your level of faith-based optimism high. In other words, you simply cannot allow what "wrecks" you to wreck you.

You can't let the "discontent" part of your holy discontent discourage or depress you. Trust me: I was almost sidelined on two separate occasions by my own passion pursuits in ministry and had to learn the (very) hard way that, regardless of the pain, the risk, the disappointment, or the setbacks associated with feeding your holy discontent, you simply *cannot* let hope die.

One of the most valuable lessons coming out of those ultra-difficult seasons was that I am the only one who can keep my hope meter high. Likewise, only *you* can keep your hope meter high. In other words, it's an issue of *self-leadership*. Sure, it would be nice to outsource that little task to your boss, your friend, your family member, your mentor, your teacher, your colleague, or your pastor, but in the end, they cannot do it for you; it's between you and God alone.

If you find your hope waning, let me offer you two suggestions for how to reinspire it for the road ahead.

First, assess your level of belief in your holy discontent. If your holy discontent revolves around building an outreach-oriented church, then ask yourself, "Do I still have a deep-seated belief that lost people really can get found?" If your holy discontent deals with children's ministry, then ask yourself, "Do I honestly believe that, after a few years of healthy care and attention, even badly abused kids can heal?" If it centers on women's services, ask, "Do I believe that unemployed, single moms really can get back on their feet?" If it involves relief efforts in Africa, ask, "Do I believe—really, truly believe—that poor people can be lifted out of generational poverty?"

If your answer is no, then I highly recommend scrapping whatever plans you had for today and getting alone with God instead. Beg him to pump you *full* of Spirit-inspired, holy-discontent-driven, refuse-to-be-shaken belief! You owe it to yourself—and to the people around you—to re-establish your belief *each and every day*.

The second way to rebuild hope is to check your life for energy leaks. Is all your vigor sucked dry by the time you can even *consider* pursuing a real passion pursuit? Are you devoting your entire supply of fuel to petty causes? Are you spending inordinate time in the squeaky relational wheels that occupy your world?

Friends, when a leader's shoulders sag, everyone else's shoulders begin to sag too. If your shoulders are drooping, it won't be long before you find everyone around you hunched over and beaten down. You hold *tremendous* responsibility in this regard, because when hope dies in a leader, the game ends and the cause is defeated. Please don't let this happen to you!

This area of self-leadership—the issue of keeping your energy high—is absolutely critical because everyone you lead, whether a friend, a child, an employee, takes their cue from you. I'll say it again: *everyone* takes their cue from you.

The good news is this: When you charge toward your holy discontent with boundless passion, optimism, and energy, you become the very best kind of contagious! It's positive magnetic living in its purest form. And you just never know what God will do with a few folks who band together and get determined about pulling the very best thoughts, ideas, and actions out of each other toward fixing whatever is broken in the world. Erwin McManus says that it is in *this* context that true greatness gets unleashed.[1]

Getting It Right

There is so much at stake here in our broken world. As you draw your own conclusions about our modern-day state of affairs, I wonder if you are willing for God to speak to you in regard to your own holy discontent. Are you willing for God to lead you in the endeavor of figuring out what it is that you cannot stand—what wrecks you from the inside out?

Don't forget that there's a reason why you grew up the way you did. Why you've experienced what you have. Why you've traveled where you've been. And he is looking for someone *just like you* to start setting some things right in this world.

Maybe you know exactly what that holy discontent is. I urge you to commit to praying for more clarity regarding the vision God might birth out of it. Whatever you do, declare today that you will jump all over the task of feeding it!

Or perhaps you once were gripped by a firestorm of frustration that compelled you to kingdom-building action, but you've let the dream die. I encourage you to revisit what it was that got you in the game to begin with. Head back to the burning-bush conversation that directed you all those years ago.

Or you might be one who simply needs to stick your neck out and grab onto a higher level of risk. You need to step into the "fundamental state" where you can be refreshed regarding the high stakes of effecting change and where you can be inspired to ratchet everything up a notch in pursuit of a worthy vision.

Friends, in what *other* life are you going to go all out? We all have one shot and one shot only to leave a lasting legacy—a definitive mark on this world that reflects our decision to lean into, not away from, our areas of holy discontent. A legacy that says, "I have been trusted to carry God's message of hope to an aching, fractured world in need, and I refuse to rest until my role in that is fulfilled."

When we get this stuff right, we show the rest of the world that the present state of affairs does *not* determine the possibilities life holds. We can finish differently than we started, friends. We can.

We *can*.

●

Every year, I take some time in December to assess the twelve months that have just passed. This exercise for the year 2005 was especially impactful as I pinpointed the greatest moments of celebration as well as the toughest situations I'd faced. There were some *very* difficult days that were extremely sobering to revisit. But there were also some huge "ups" for me, such as Willow's thirtieth anniversary.

When I really thought about it, though, there was only one moment in the entire year that qualified for the time when I was *most* hope-filled, the *most* inspired, and the *most* connected with God, if you want to describe it that way. A friend gave me a framed photo recently that I keep in my office. It's a picture of a walk I took while on a video shoot in Africa—without a doubt, my "highest high" of 2005.

Willow does a lot of work with various partners on the continent of Africa, and early in the month of December, I was filming a brief video that would air on the giant screens in our main auditorium just before Christmas to enlist additional support for eradicating the pains of this HIV/AIDS pandemic. We were shooting footage in a little village in Zambia—the same village where Jude serves, actually—that Willow Creek people have started generously supporting with a food program. There are kids who would literally die without the "mealy meal" we have been able to supply; aside from that, they receive no consistent food day in and day out.

One day during the shoot, I went to the food distribution office to help volunteers hand out bags of mealy meal. I saw a young widow with four little children hovering around her, two of whom, I discovered, were AIDS orphans now in her care. It was well above 90 degrees outside, and she had already stood in the midday sun for four or five hours, hot and sticky, just waiting on her bag of food.

Each of those bags weighed upwards of fifty pounds, and just eyeing this frail woman, she couldn't have been an ounce over eighty-five herself. As I stood there watching the line inch forward, I wondered how on earth she was going to be able to carry such a heavy load all the way home. Just then, the video crew took a short break. I turned to one of the locals who spoke some English and said, "How is that woman going to get her bag home?"

"She'll pull it," he said. "Or they'll find some other way ... there's *five* of them, you know."

That seemed preposterous to me. "I'm on break," I told him as I saw the woman drop the bag onto the ground and begin dragging it down the unpaved road. "Why don't I just carry it for her?"

"She lives a *long* way away," came the response.

I grinned at him as I jogged off to catch up with the woman. "You underestimate me!"

I could hear his good-natured laugh in the distance as I reached the woman and her kids. I bent down, grabbed the bag of maize — it was a heck of a lot heavier than it looked! — and hoisted the thing onto my shoulder. "I'd be happy to carry this for you," I said. "Is this okay?"

She seemed relieved as we started down the dirt path toward her home.

With each step, I tried to take in everything around me. The narrow road was packed with women balancing woven baskets and tall piles of thatch and smaller bags of grain on top of their heads. Every few hundred feet, I would see women stooped over rusty spigots, trying to wash the dust and grime out of their clothes with no soap and with water that most likely was contaminated by disease.

There were scores of children wandering around, even the youngest of them carrying papooses on their backs with quiet infants stuffed inside. There are few adults around to pay attention to babies who cry, and so children in this village are strangely silent. I looked into their jet-black eyes as I walked with the heavy bag of mealy meal slumped over my shoulder, and all my heart could say was, "Oh, man. These kids—they are *all* precious in his sight."

It was so sobering, that trek from the food distribution center to a meager hut more than a mile away. I kept thinking, *In the most literal meaning possible, the difference between life and death for this family is on my shoulders*. I was humbled like I've never been humbled before. In a way I'd not previously experienced, I felt *in cadence* with Christ, if that makes sense. I said over and over to no one in particular, "This is good, Bill ... this is good. I know there are a million things you could be pouring your energy into right now, but please don't miss this moment, because this is something that your heart needs to be tenderized by."

●

We finally arrived at her hut and as I sat with the family for a few minutes to say a prayer and to try to put words to my earnest concern regarding the daily suffering they were experiencing. As we talked there in the stifling heat with dozens of curious onlookers wandering around, I was overcome with gratitude for all that God had already done in that village.

I saw bicycles our folks had donated so that AIDS care-givers could get to more people in a given day. I saw stacks upon stacks of mealy meal bags, just waiting to be placed in grateful hands. I saw children in uniforms who were finally receiving a solid education. And I firmly believe the day will come when poverty in Samfya—in all its forms—will be a thing of the past.

In the most unexpected of places, and while doing the most unexpected of tasks, God had revealed a level of soul satisfaction I'd not soon sense again.

Life That Is Truly Life

Along the path of pursuing your holy discontent, whether it winds along a dusty road in the most forsaken part of Zambia or through the heart of downtown Detroit or down the manicured streets of a suburban neighborhood, you too will inevitably experience transcendent moments that surprise you with their power and ability to satisfy your soul.

Here's how I know: there's a short passage in 1 Timothy that says, "Command them to do good, to be rich in good deeds, and to be generous and willing to share. In this way they will lay up treasure for themselves as a firm foundation for the coming age, so that they may take hold of the *life that is truly life.*"[2]

Life that is truly life: that's it! That is exactly what I was feeling when I had that bag of mealy meal slung over my shoulder. I was completely aligned with what God would have me do in that moment. I felt totally in step with heaven and totally present on earth. I realized I was living life that was really life, a sensation that can come over anyone—a faithful husband, a devoted mom, a fierce advocate for the poor, a precise construction worker, an honorable lawyer, or a generous businessman alike.

Friends, this is what it means to live out of your holy discontent, being where you're supposed to be, doing exactly what you're supposed to do. And each time you get a little taste of those good works getting accomplished in your midst, you'll shout out, "This is it! I'm living it. I'm living the life that is really life!"

Folks within earshot may look at you a little strangely because they don't fully get why you do what you do. But in your heart, you will say to yourself, *For some strange reason, this is life that is truly life for me! This is why I'm still sucking air down here. This is the activistic expression of my deepest holy discontent.*

And I wouldn't trade it for anything.

Postscript:
It Doesn't Have to End Like This

In the spring of 2005 I was asked to speak at one of the toughest funeral experiences of my life. Many years ago my son, Todd, befriended a young man in South Haven named Clark. Over time our two families became quite close, and we grew to care deeply for Clark and his four brothers, as well as for their wonderful parents.

Through Todd's quiet witness and constant prayers, the day finally came when Clark trusted Christ with his life. All of us watched as the transformational power of God began to unfold in his life—it was unbelievable! As Clark's faith grew, he became increasingly interested in working in full-time ministry, but regardless which path he chose to take, it was clear that Clark was a sharp kid with an incredibly promising future.

But that would all change one night on a country road.

The day after Clark's terrible automobile collision, his family asked if I would speak at his funeral. They truly are some of the finest people I've ever had the pleasure of meeting, and all I could think about was what an honor it would be to serve them during this excruciatingly painful time in their lives.

As the day of Clark's funeral neared, I pleaded with God to give me grace-filled words to comfort the parents, family, and the several hundred friends who would be there. Although Clark had made the decision to follow Christ, none of his family members were too active on the spiritual front. As far as I knew, their last real church involvement hadn't been for over two decades. I knew that my comments would either help point them toward God or hinder them from ever seeking after anything spiritual. As you'd guess, I was feeling the pressure to get this just right.

With God's help, I managed to get through my portion of the heart-wrenching experience before we all drove to the local cemetery for the gravesite service. For some reason, as my wife and kids and I walked toward the dark green canopy that hovered above Clark's grave, I felt a distinct prompting from God to "stay alert," to listen closely to *every* word spoken, and to be ready for anything that might unfold at the cemetery that day. It was just a whisper, really, but it was undeniably the Holy Spirit talking.

The family all sat underneath the tent on chairs, which faced the casket, as hundreds of onlookers pressed themselves into concentric circles around them. The finality of

Clark's death started to overtake the family just as a pastor-friend of theirs stood to begin delivering his comments.

Lynne was on one side of me, a grief-stricken Todd on the other. In the midst of trying to console my family—and myself—I continued to hear with crystal clarity the Spirit saying, "Stay ready, Bill. Stay ready."

It made no sense to me, this prompting, because technically, my part of the funeral was over. I reengaged with the pastor's remarks just as he began to recite the liturgy about ashes to ashes and dust to dust from a small book he held in his hands. As he concluded his comments, the casket was gently lowered into the ground.

In a matter of minutes, the whole thing was over. Clark was gone—just like that.

The crowd collectively took a deep breath, unsure of what to do or say in the awkward silence. Without any warning, the family suddenly came undone. They couldn't contain the enormity of their pent-up grief any longer, and all you could hear throughout the cemetery were sobs from a family whose hearts had just been ripped out. Before long, the waves of men, women, and children spilling over the boundary lines of that canopy were crying as well. I stood there stunned, just like the rest of the guests. No one knew what to think or how to help. Everyone knew that the ceremony was officially over. But no one could move. *No* one. Something just didn't seem right.

After what seemed an eternity, Clark's dad rose to his feet, walked around the grave, and began scanning the crowd that surrounded him. When he caught my eye, he walked directly toward me, wrapped his arms around my back, and cried on my shoulder. Through his quiet sobs, he whispered, "Bill, it just can't end like this. Please! It just can't end like this!"

In that instant, I realized why the Spirit had asked me to stay alert.

I took a long breath and walked Clark's dad back to his chair. I collected myself and then said simply, "Mr. Spencer has asked if we could all pray one more prayer."

You could have heard a pin drop.

My mouth opened, and I began talking to God in the plainest, most earnest terms I could think of. I hadn't prepared for this prayer, but God kept putting words in my mind just as I needed them. They were promise-filled words. Hope-filled words. They were bold words that told Clark's family and friends that because of the resurrection of Jesus Christ and Clark's faith in Christ, his soul had already crossed over to the other side. That he was already in the presence of God! And that in Christ he and his family and friends could actually be reunited for eternity and that people from every walk of life and every sort of past could have a brand new future, secured in God's eternal presence. "The doors of the kingdom are open ...," I told them that day as I prayed passionately for several minutes, "... to every single person here."

●

That afternoon, during a reception for the family, Clark's dad must have thanked me five separate times for infusing hope into people at the gravesite service. "It just couldn't end like that, Bill ... it just *couldn't* end like that," he kept saying.

I knew he was right.

The night of Clark's funeral, I drifted off to sleep with six words ringing in my ears. They were the words that Clark's dad had whispered to me through his tears: "It just can't end like this!"

It just can't end like this.

I don't know about you, but in those six words I hear an unmistakable cry for hope. And our whole broken, sorry world is whispering something similar to all of us who name the name of Christ these days. "Does it have to end like this?"

Our world is wondering, Will darkness and evil prevail? Will tyrants always rule? Will terrorists keep wreaking havoc? Will AIDS only continue to spread? Does it have to end like this?

Will poverty just increase? Will racism win the day? Will violence and war persist? Will hunger and homelessness keep multiplying? Will churches keep closing their doors and posting "For Sale" signs? Will marriages keep breaking up? Will depression continue robbing people of joy? Does it have to end like this?

Is this really the human lot?

Is this all that life's about?

Is this really how it will all end?

Does it *have* to end like this?

I happen to believe that those who whisper these questions deserve our *very* best response, friends. And although I don't know what you might say to their questions, I certainly know what I say: "*No!* It absolutely does *not* have to end like this! It really doesn't."

If I believe *anything*, it's that in Christ, through Christ, and because of Christ, it most certainly doesn't have to end like this! Let me remind you—you who are fellow Christ-followers—that we steward the only message on planet Earth that can give people what their hearts need most, which is hope.

Hope that sins can be forgiven. Hope that prayers can be answered. Hope that doors of opportunity that seem locked can be opened. Hope that broken relationships can be reconciled. Hope that diseased bodies can be healed. Hope that damaged trust can be restored. Hope that dead churches can be resurrected.

In other words, it really doesn't have to end like this.

Of *all* people, we must claim that hope and live in it and radiate it to others. And we must proclaim that message of hope to everyone God gives us the opportunity to influence. That's partly why God entrusts us with the ability to provide energy and courage and creative thought to the people around us who so desperately need it through the activity of pursuing our holy discontent ... so that hope won't die. So that we can look our weary friends and downcast family members in the eye and say, "It doesn't have to end like this. Because with Christ in the equation, it can end much better."

Figure out what you can't stand. Channel your holy discontent energy into helping to fix what's broken in this life. Let your passion pursuits shout to the world, "It really doesn't have to end like this!

"Just watch. . . ."

I value your thoughts about what you've just read.
Please share them with me. You'll find contact information
in the back of this book.

Notes

Chapter 1: The Question That Started It All

1. networkforgood.org/volunteer/volunteertradition.aspx
2. eu-esis.org/Basic/ATbasic00.htm
3. Exodus 2:11.
4. Exodus 2:12a.
5. From Exodus 3:7–10.
6. John 8:32.
7. Luke 3:14, Philippians 4:11–12, 1 Timothy 6:6–8, Hebrews 13:5.

Chapter 2: Popeye People

1. redcross.org/services/disaster
2. nobelprize.org/peace/laureates/1964/king-acceptance.html
3. CNN Washington, 1984 (cnn.com/WORLD/9709/mother.teresa/impact/index.html), emphasis added.
4. en.wikipedia.org/wiki/Mother_Teresa

5. CARS stands for "Christian Automotive Repairmen Serving." Started in the late 1980s, they remain committed to meeting the transportation needs of people who are unable to meet those needs themselves.

6. William MacDonald, *Believer's Bible Commentary*, Acts 2:43 (Nashville: Nelson, 1995), 1588.

7. en.wikipedia.org/wiki/World_Vision

8. worldvision.org

9. billygraham.org/News_Article.asp?ArticleID=104

10. Harold Myra and Marshall Shelley, *The Leadership Secrets of Billy Graham* (Grand Rapids, Mich.: Zondervan, 2005), 318.

11. bgea.com

Chapter 3: Your "One Thing"

1. TNIV (emphasis mine).

2. 2 Corinthians 3:18.

3. Max Lucado, *Cure for the Common Life: Living in Your Sweet Spot* (Nashville: W Publishing Group, 2005), 2.

Chapter 4: Feeding the Frustration

1. Galatians 6:9 KJV.

Chapter 5: A Worthy Fight

1. Steven Kasher, *The Civil Rights Movement: A Photographic History, 1954–68* (New York: Abbeville Press, 1996).

Chapter 6: Wherever It Takes You, Whenever It Takes You There

1. Nehemiah 1:3b MSG.

2. Nehemiah 1:3a MSG.

3. Nehemiah 1:4.

4. Michka Assayas, *Bono: In Conversation with Michka Assayas* (New York: Riverhead Books, 2005), 224.

5. one.org

6. data.org/archives/000774.php

7. Assayas, *Bono*, 215.

8. James 1:27.

Chapter 7: Magnetic Living

1. Robert E. Quinn, *Building the Bridge as You Walk on It* (San Francisco: Jossey-Bass, 2004), 36 (emphasis mine).

2. Quinn, *Building the Bridge*, 21.

3. From Proverbs 31:8–9 and Psalm 82:3, NIV.

Chapter 8: Hope's Purpose

1. Erwin McManus, *The Barbarian Way* (Nashville: Nelson, 2005), 134.

2. 1 Timothy 6:18–19 (emphasis mine).

Resources

Ready to discover your holy discontent? Perhaps one of these organizations will head you in the right direction.

- American Red Cross—redcross.org
- DATA (Debt AIDS Trade Africa)—data.org
- Good Sense Ministry—goodsenseministry.com
- Habitat for Humanity—habitat.org
- ONE, The Campaign to Make Poverty History—one.org
- Volunteers of America—voa.org
- The WCA Leadership Summit—willowcreek.com/conferences
- World Vision—worldvision.org
- Your local church!

WILLOW
Willow Creek Association

Willow Creek Association
Vision, Training, Resources for Prevailing Churches

This resource was created to serve you and to help you build a local church that prevails. It is just one of many ministry tools that are part of the Willow Creek Resources® line, published by the Willow Creek Association together with Zondervan.

The Willow Creek Association (WCA) was created in 1992 to serve a rapidly growing number of churches from across the denominational spectrum that are committed to helping unchurched people become fully devoted followers of Christ. Membership in the WCA now numbers over 12,000 Member Churches worldwide from more than ninety denominations.

The Willow Creek Association links like-minded Christian leaders with each other and with strategic vision, training, and resources in order to help them build prevailing churches designed to reach their redemptive potential. Here are some of the ways the WCA does that.

- **A2: Building Prevailing Acts 2 Churches—Today**—an annual two-and-a-half day event, held at Willow Creek Community Church in South Barrington, Illinois, to explore strategies for building churches that reach out to seekers and build believers, and to discover new innovations and breakthroughs from Acts 2 churches around the country.

- **The Leadership Summit**—a once a year, two-and-a-half-day conference to envision and equip Christians with leadership gifts and responsibilities. Presented live at Willow Creek as well as via satellite broadcast to over one hundred locations across North America, this event is designed to increase the leadership effectiveness of pastors, ministry staff, volunteer church leaders, and Christians in the marketplace.

- **Ministry-Specific Conferences**—throughout each year the WCA hosts a variety of conferences and training events—both at Willow Creek's main campus and offsite, across the U.S., and around the world—targeting church leaders and volunteers in ministry-specific areas such as: evangelism, small groups, preaching and teaching, the arts, children, students, women, volunteers, stewardship, raising up resources, etc.

- **Willow Creek Resources®**—provides churches with trusted and field-tested ministry resources in such areas as leadership, evangelism, spiritual formation, spiritual gifts, small groups, stewardship, student ministry, children's ministry, the use of the arts—drama, media, contemporary music—and more.

- **WCA Member Benefits**—includes substantial discounts to WCA training events, a 20 percent discount on all Willow Creek Resources®, *Defining Moments* monthly audio journal for leaders, quarterly *Willow* magazine, access to a Members-Only section on WillowNet, monthly communications, and more. Member Churches also receive special discounts and premier services through WCA's growing number of ministry partners—Select Service Providers—and save an average of $500 annually depending on the level of engagement.

For specific information about WCA conferences, resources, membership, and other ministry services contact:

Willow Creek Association
P.O. Box 3188
Barrington, IL 60011-3188
Phone: 847-570-9812
Fax: 847-765-5046
www.willowcreek.com